Praise for We Did It Here!

We Did It Here! is a treasure trove of hope for building successful schools. This outstanding lessons in leadership is brilliantly written by Brin Best. At the beginning of the 21st Century we are often encouraged to 'work outside the box', a very worthy expression of innovative intent. This book offers up much more than dreams and intentions, this is the stuff of current realities. It contains solid evidence of learners and leaders working not just 'in the box' and 'out of the box', but out to the very corners of the box and the space it sits in. Charged with positive energy, and balanced with rigorous research, this book explores the ways in which contemporary schools are serving their learners at the cutting edge of practice. This is a must-read for every teacher, senior leader and aspirant manager, not to mention an uplifting and stimulating read for anyone with an interest in teaching and learning. This beautifully considered work provides the rules for success for an effective school. It celebrates effective practice and goes on to eloquently challenge the existing system and lay down tracks for the next 50 years of educational history.

>Will Thomas
>Education Performance Coach, Author of Coaching Solutions

There are few things as reassuring and compelling to teachers and school leaders as case studies of success. All the theory in the world is outweighed by one story that educationalists can relate to in their own context. Brin Best has produced a range of compelling stories which give detailed guidance on how schools have addressed some of the most challenging issues of today. Each study provides credible examples of actual strategies that have worked. The narrative is accompanied by a range of supportive materials and is underpinned by detailed and systematic analysis, explanation and discussion. This is a practical resource that allows schools to explore the possibilities of change.

>John West-Burnham
>Visiting Professor of Education, University of Bristol

As Harold McAlindon once said: Do not follow where the path may lead. Go instead where there is no path and leave a trail. This book celebrates some innovative trailblazers without alienating the less adventurous. It provides creative ideas broken down into 'doable' chunks, and is liberally peppered with a 'can-do' attitude. I hope that government are receptive to Brin's challenge to nurture creativity within our system. The more that follow the excellent ideas in the book, the happier our society will be.

> David Harris
> Author of *Are You Dropping The Baton* and Principal (designate) of Nottingham University Samworth Academy

If I were a secondary Head Teacher I would want to keep a copy of We Did It Here! in full sight to remind me just what schools should be about; if I were a classroom teacher, I would want a copy to remind me just why I came in to teaching; and if I were training to be a teacher, I would want it to show me just what I was aiming for. Prepared to be inspired and uplifted!

A must for all secondary school leaders and governors.

> Lyn Bull
> Independent Education Consultant

Inspirational Stories of School
Improvement and Classroom Change

We Did It Here!

Brin Best

Crown House Publishing Limited
www.crownhouse.co.uk
www.chpus.com

First published by Crown House Publishing Ltd
Crown Buildings, Bancyfelin, Carmarthen, Wales, SA33 5ND, UK
www.crownhouse.co.uk

and Crown House Publishing Company LLC
6 Trowbridge Drive, Suite 5, Bethel, CT 06801, USA
www.chpus.com

© Brin Best 2008

The right of Brin Best to be identified as the author of this work has been asserted by him in accordance with the Copyright, Designs and Patents Act 1988.

All rights reserved. Except as permitted under current legislation no part of this work may be photocopied, stored in a retrieval system, published, performed in public, adapted, broadcast, transmitted, recorded or reproduced in any form or by any means, without the prior permission of the copyright owners. Enquiries should be addressed to Crown House Publishing Limited.

Page 26: Image reproduced with permission of the Lancaster Guardian

British Library of Cataloguing-in-Publication Data
A catalogue entry for this book is available from the British Library.

International Standard Book Number
978-184590089-2

Library of Congress Control Number
2007938975

Printed and bound in the UK: Gomes Press, Llandysul

Contents

	Acknowledgements	1
	Introduction	3
Chapter 1	On Home Ground Settle High School and Community College	7
Chapter 2	Scholarship and Care in the Shadow of the Fells Queen Elizabeth School, Kirkby Lonsdale	45
Chapter 3	Transforming a School in Challenging Circumstances Northumberland Park Community School	77
Chapter 4	Let's Focus on Learning Matthew Moss High School, Rochdale	103
Chapter 5	An Enterprising School? St Nicholas Catholic High School, Northwich	129
Chapter 6	Regenerating Education through Partnership Dearne Valley Education Partnership	161
Chapter 7	Stories from Successful Classrooms and Departments	181
Chapter 8	Learning the Lessons	207
Chapter 9	A Manifesto for Real Change in our Schools	227
	About the author	253
	Further reading and information	255
	Index	257

Acknowledgements

I owe a huge debt of gratitude to the staff working in the schools featured in this book. They have without reservation welcomed me with open arms, have been eager to tell me about their schools and have been extremely generous with their knowledge. They have reaffirmed my belief that this country is blessed with some of the finest teachers and school leaders in the world.

I want to pay a special tribute to those teachers and leaders who have chosen to remain anonymous in this book. I would have preferred to have named them so their work can be attributed properly, but their inspiring stories can only be told if their identities are kept secret, for reasons that will remain clear as you read them. It's probably fitting that such dedicated education professionals have waived their right to be identified publicly in the hope that others, perhaps in similar circumstances, can be empowered by their testimonies. I take some comfort from knowing their outstanding efforts are generally recognised in their own schools.

I have also benefited greatly from countless conversations with young people attending the featured schools. Their confident and positive outlook is testament to the exceptional work of the staff in their schools, a fact that many of them are happy to go on record to confirm. Thanks are also due to Dan Varney, Isabella Donnelly, Macia Grebot and Clare Smale, who kindly brought to my attention some of the schools and teachers featured.

I would also like to thank various people who have helped to shape the book as it has unfolded. I have especially benefited from the ideas of Gill O'Donnell, with whom I have worked closely for many years. Her creative approach and willingness to ask appropriate questions at the right time have been warmly appreciated. Gill also read the entire manuscript and made a number of helpful suggestions. I also thank Alan Cranston, Linda Edge, Will Thomas and Jane West who provided valuable additional ideas, especially in relation to the final chapter.

As well as contributing a valuable chapter in her own right, Sophie Craven made some timely contributions at a critical stage during the planning of the project, and provided helpful comments on the final two chapters. Her ability to think incisively to find new insights and understandings never fails to amaze me, and has contributed significantly to the coherency of the finished book.

Finally I would like to thank David Bowman and his staff at Crown House Publishing for having the faith and vision to publish a book such as this. It is indeed rare to find a publisher who is prepared to produce unconventional titles that try to address burning issues in education.

Introduction

I first started to think about this book during a train journey across northern England on a grey February day in 2005. I was making my way from my home in Yorkshire to work with a group of school leaders and teachers who had proved negative on my previous meeting with them. Though I always try to remain cheerful in the face of challenges, I was expecting this to be another difficult day.

Following ten years working in the classroom, and in an advisory capacity in education authorities, I've been supporting teachers in a consultancy role for the last five years. I've also been writing about teaching, learning and school improvement, and carrying out research into effective schools. I had enjoyed tremendously my time in the classroom and was rewarded on many levels, but my move into consultancy work had been fuelled by a desire to work alongside education professionals to develop and share good practice more widely. It has been a privilege to witness the work of hundreds of schools over the years and it has given me the chance to understand what can and cannot work in a range of settings. The whole experience has been terrifically uplifting.

So why was I so hesitant about the training session I was leading that day? In short, because I had become rather tired of hearing teachers say 'You couldn't do that here!' Much of my work centres on helping schools to implement changes that enable them to improve and this often requires me to talk about how other people have achieved success in their schools. My heartfelt belief is that we can *all* achieve life-changing things in our schools if we *believe* we can and then carry out creative and determined actions to achieve our goals. But on that February day I was expecting to hear those familiar negative rebuffs when I suggested new ways of thinking and doing that went outside teachers' comfort zones—and I wasn't looking forward to this negativity.

Change and constancy

We are truly living in changing times in education—from advances in ICT that are transforming how learning and teachers are viewed, to the overhaul of the professional roles of teachers and others working in schools, for which we have yet to see the full ramifications. Perhaps one constant, however, is that the teachers and school leaders in our country remain an incredibly dedicated group of professionals in the face of these constant changes. But they can also be a sceptical, stubborn and frustrating bunch of people to work with too. Perhaps blinkered by the constraints of their school, department or classroom— or by the external pressures which affect them—they sometimes choose not to embrace the exciting possibilities of change. When they do this their own well-being and, more worryingly still, that of their students suffers.

I made an important decision as I travelled across England that day. I realised I had to begin another journey: a mission to seek out successful schools in diverse settings and to document their stories more fully. My hope was that others would be inspired by the power of what these schools have achieved—empowered to realise that it really is possible to make inspirational things happen in *every* school. I am fortunate to have enjoyed successes in a range of classrooms, departments and schools, and have received some awards and other accolades for my education work. I feel I understand quite well some of the factors that lead to success in schools and what others can do to create a brighter future in their own institutions. But I realised that this alone was not going to be enough to convince some people that it is possible to achieve their dreams in their schools too. Instead, I had to gather testimonies from schools just like theirs; from people just like them. And as I mulled over the schools I knew that fitted the bill, I realised that the journey had already begun in my mind, a journey that ends with the book you're now reading.

The scope and organisation of the book

In order to find suitable schools to feature I have toured the country and scoured the literature to find a wide range of schools, travelling to rural areas, leafy suburbs and inner city settings. I was eager to avoid those schools that were especially privileged in some way and have avoided those already well-documented schools that some would claim have an unfair advantage, due to a combination of funding, social advantage or some other preferential characteristics. Instead, many of the schools featured have emerged from *challenging circumstances* to achieve success. Whatever school issues are currently occupying your mind, be sure that at least one of the schools featured has also confronted—and overcome—that issue.

The book focuses on secondary schools. This is not because I believe that the ideas presented here are unique to the secondary phase; instead I simply feel that after fifteen years of intensive work in secondaries I understand their needs quite well. But I would maintain that there are important principles applicable to colleagues working in primary schools too.

The main part of the book is taken up with the stories of a diverse range of schools. There is also a chapter outlining what a range of teachers and subject leaders have done in their own classrooms and departments, plus a chapter on a collaborative approach to education. But I wanted to do more than just tell the stories of these schools— I wanted to reflect on their success and ponder how as a nation we could embed similar success into all our schools. I bring the book to a conclusion, therefore, with two more analytical chapters. The first, 'Learning the Lessons', tries to bring together the key messages from the schools featured—my aim is to crystallise what it is that distinguishes schools that are successful in achieving their goals. My hope is that this big picture look at success in schools can provide a helpful framework against which you can test your own ideas and thinking—or even use as a stepping stone for success. The second part of this chapter explores the barriers to innovation in our schools. Here, I explore why it is that more schools do not feel able to embrace creative change in the manner of the schools featured. By understanding these barriers, it should be possible to determine what needs to be done to help schools overcome them.

I draw the book to a close with a ten point 'Manifesto for Real Change'. I believe passionately that as a nation we should provide the conditions that would allow the widest cross section of school leaders and teachers to embrace creative approaches, thereby building brighter futures for our young people. At the same time I sometimes cringe at the number of hurdles and 'new initiatives' thrown at schools by governments which can seem hungry for change at the cost of real progress. In this final chapter, therefore, I outline what I feel needs to be done at a national, regional and local level that would surely allow more educational professionals to say 'We did it here!' This includes suggested actions for schools, the government and wider society.

As well as providing evidence and testimonies that show what is possible in schools, I hope the book will also be seen as a celebration of good practice in education in the first decade of the twenty-first century. My hope, of course, is that you will find the stories and testimonies in this book inspiring. But I would have failed if you do not also find them empowering. No matter what challenges you are facing, given whatever special circumstances your school finds itself in, there are key messages of support and hope in this book. And if you're ever flagging as you tackle your priorities head on, remember this—the young people who you currently work with, the decision-makers of tomorrow, will not get another chance at their education. For this reason alone I hope you'll read the book, gather your resources and face whatever tomorrow throws at you with renewed enthusiasm—and a belief that you *can* make a difference.

Brin Best
Otley, West Yorkshire

Chapter 1

On Home Ground

> 'A sense of community comes not from acknowledging common ground, but from realizing what makes us different from others, then working together in order to understand, celebrate and eventually enjoy others' differences so they may become part of us.' Jarvis Hayes

I'm going to begin by reflecting on some of the successes enjoyed by the school where I taught for most of my teaching career. As I try to document and analyse success in this book it seems sensible to start with the school I know best, a school whose challenges and achievements were part of my day to day life for the best part of a decade. Though there are several aspects of the school that would be worthy of mention, one area clearly stands out and this will be the focus of this first chapter.

While some school names evolve over time and have no special significance, the insertion of the word 'Community' into Settle High School's nameplate was a very significant development. It heralded the beginning of concerted effort to place this rural comprehensive school at the heart of its community. But let me start with a little background on the school in order to paint a picture of life as a teacher and student at Settle High School and Community College during the 1990s.

As competition for students gathers pace it is not unusual for schools to draw in young people from ever-wider catchment areas. But few schools can match the 400 square mile influence of the only 13–18 state secondary school in North Yorkshire. About a third of its 600 students come from farming backgrounds and most of the others have parents who are touched by the other chief component of the local economy—tourism. The school itself is perched on the banks of the River Ribble on the outskirts of town, overlooked by impressive limestone peaks which were ground into a multitude of shapes by the glaciers which sculpted this part of the Yorkshire Dales. It's a beautiful place in which to teach and learn.

Although the school day starts early in Settle (registration begins at 8.30 a.m.) it is not unusual to be teaching children who have already been at work for three hours by the time the bell signals the end of the first lesson—especially during lambing time. The school recognises and celebrates its rural heritage in a range of ways. Rural studies qualifications have been a firm favourite for decades; crops and flowers are grown by students; farm animals are kept on the grounds. I remember vividly a geography lesson in March which was interrupted by the appearance of a lost lamb at my classroom door! This is a rural school and proud of it.

The school has always played an important community role, not least because its students often do not get the chance to meet much outside school hours—their farms or villages may be separated by wide valleys or barren peaks. The school has, therefore, long served as a point of focus in the community and is a place in which people gather and work together, especially in times of need.

'Through its work within the community it plays an important role in the life and work of the area, and of its students'

Ofsted report, January 2003

No one was prepared, however, for the impact that the foot-and-mouth crisis of 2000 was to have on the rural hinterland of Settle. The foundations of the community were rocked by the financial hardship, widespread animal culling and sense of blackness that descended on the area during those exhausting times at the height of the outbreak. Foot-and-mouth disease also brought division to the community: the haves and the have-nots. Sitting side by side in a classroom one day was a child who could still tend their flock of pedigree Ribblesdale sheep, next to his friend who was facing up to the massacre of their family's 100-year-old dairy herd. In looking forward to the challenges that twenty-first century education would bring to the area, the realisation dawned that in order to continue to be successful, the school would need to play its part in healing rifts as well as cementing bonds within the wider community.

> 'Farming locally was severely affected by the foot-and-mouth outbreak in 2001 and its repercussions are still being felt in the area'
>
> Ofsted report, January 2003

In the remainder of this chapter, I present examples of the some of the activities that the school organised during an eight year period. It is important to place on record that the activities outlined below were not necessarily designed specifically or solely in order to bring the school closer to its community, though this was certainly an important feature of all of them. I do not wish to give the impression that the school's efforts were strategically focused *just* on the community or indeed that a strict master plan guided the things mentioned on a day to day basis; indeed some of the activities just seemed to happen by chance. Nevertheless, together they amount to a series of activities which, combined with the associated communications work described, helped the school to become a leader in its community work.

One thousand make a difference

While many schools plan community activities that try to involve students in their delivery, few strive to ensure that *every* student on the roll plays a part. And fewer still try to do that by bringing the sights and sounds of the farmyard to the school, complete with a herd of Jersey cows and a flock of Wensleydale sheep. Yet the Settle Environment Fair of 2000 had these far reaching targets as two of its central goals. Over the course of a memorable day in June the school was transformed into a vibrant learning resource for over a thousand children from feeder primary schools. Young people in the area still talk about what they did and saw on that wonderful summer's day.

This highly innovative event was staged as a follow up to a science fair in 1999 that had been awarded a £10,000 grant from the Royal Society. The science fair had given staff and students the confidence to try things out, together with experience in managing large numbers of children. The following year staff wanted to take things further and celebrate the rural heritage of the school. The Environment Fair of millennium year was sponsored by the charity Human Scale Education, Hanson Aggregates and Skipton Building Society, who together provided the funding and advice that enabled the event to go ahead on such a large scale.

A working group of enthusiastic staff and students had met frequently in the months leading up to the day in order to lay the foundations for the event. There was a lot of planning and preparation to get through. Creative approaches to learning were to be a focus for the event, with staff and students taking a lead role in running workshops in equal proportion. A notable feature of the project was how the whole school pulled together to make things happen—there was a tangible feeling that this was a vision worth working towards. Staff and students worked extremely hard in the days running up to the event to ensure its success—outstanding educational opportunities do not happen by accident.

A noteworthy feature of the day was the active involvement of all subject departments. But interestingly, many staff were eager to cast off traditional subject constraints to work in areas they were not used to. Hence there were science teachers involved in theatre, PE teachers going river dipping, geography teachers greeting and meeting children on arrival. There was a tangible feeling of creativity surrounding the event, which clearly encouraged staff and students to go beyond their comfort zones and try something new.

The atmosphere that was created on the day was quite unique. The thrill of real life learning was written on the faces of children from surrounding villages such as Ingleton, Horton-in-Ribblesdale and Long Preston. As they participated in thought-provoking workshops on paper making or delighted in creatures discovered dipping in the river, as they crawled through elaborate installations on the motor car and a giant plant, there was a sense that a special kind of learning was taking place. Learning which was not limited by bells and the four walls of the classroom, and instead appealed to children's innate sense of wonder.

The Environment Fair, however, represented far more than one-sided learning. An important emphasis for the day was the sharing of ideas and information. All the primary school children that took part in the visits brought with them stunning project work on an environmental theme that they had carried out in preparation for the day. The school stayed open into the evening to allow parents and the wider public to enjoy this work too, and some of the workshops staged during the day were repeated.

> *'The school is popular with parents who are very supportive of the school'*
>
> Ofsted report, January 2003

The Settle Environment Fair

Ten workshops were staged during the day and staff from the feeder primary schools selected which ones they wished their children to take part in. Throughout the day as they toured the school the visiting children were accompanied by student guides from the high school who made them feel welcome, showed them where to go and were on hand to deal with any problems.

Inside a plant

Children entered the fair through a giant plant where they learnt about plant functioning with the help of year 9 students, who read poetry and gave explanations of how plants work.

Changes along a river

Children walked and slid through a representation of a river from source to mouth, complete with rocks, sound and wildlife. They spotted pollution hazards and other key features of river valleys.

Punch and Judy on the beach

This was a fun-filled drama event led by year 13 students and a governor about litter on the beach. It was a real success with visitors and turned out to be a magnet for younger children.

Paper making

During this workshop children learnt how to make paper from waste materials, aided by GCSE students.

Sculpture

Art and design students helped children to make environmentally inspired pieces of art using natural materials. A sculpture trail made by the students helped children with their ideas.

Food webs

This workshop, aimed at older children, explored the interactions between species in different environments, such as a pond, a rainforest and a savannah.

Environmental experience

An opportunity to explore the senses and enjoy nature, led by Middlewood Trust volunteers.

River dipping

A chance to catch and examine closely what lives in the River Ribble with the aid of year 12 geography students. The catch included various kinds of fish and some giant freshwater shrimps, and the children concluded that the river in Settle is very clean.

Mini-beasts

Snails, woodlice and other creepy crawlies—many children's idea of fun! Year 12 students led experiments to learn about how the mini-beasts live and how we can affect them.

'The motor'

Many children's favourite attraction—a giant crawl-through engine complete with smoke, to learn about how motor cars affect the environment. Year 9 students took a leading role in the design and organisation of this installation.

14 | We Did It Here!

Chapter 1: On Home Ground | 15

16 | We Did It Here!

'Students relate exceptionally well to each other. Everyone is included in the life of the school. They become mature, responsible individuals'

Ofsted report, January 2003

Students' views on the event

The students who organised and led some of the workshops were given the opportunity to write about their experiences in the school newsletter. Many also used these accounts in their coursework.

> 'My task was to take small groups of children from the age of seven to eight round a mini sculpture trail

that GNVQ students had set up the day before. The different sculptures included bugs made using small stone cobbles, and twigs which were glued together. One of the best sculptures was a dog made from a wire skeleton covered with moss. The sculpture I made with another student was a pattern sculpture using leaves, fixed together and circling a tree trunk, leading into a spiral of stones on the grass. I really enjoyed the day, working with different groups of children, making the sculptures.' Adam Ralph

'A teacher, another student and I ran a workshop on paper making for the primary school children. The workshop gave the children a chance to reuse paper in an environmentally friendly way—our source was waste paper which we turned into decorative pieces of artwork. All the paper used had been collected at school as offcuts and waste. The paper was sorted into different colours, then shredded, before being soaked in hot water and instant starch powder. The paper was then pulped with a liquidiser, which formed a brightlycoloured sludge. The children were shown how to drain the pulp through special fine gauze mesh, removing the excess water to form sheets of paper. They then added extra colours in the form of stripes, shapes and patterns—even flowers and grasses. All the children seemed to enjoy the workshop and getting messy—I think it was a great idea.' Lucy Gledhill

Needless to say this newsworthy and photogenic event attracted considerable media attention, both locally and nationally. However, the school also made the most of these PR opportunities by actively managing the media and arranging photo opportunities. The result was extensive coverage of the day, especially in the print media, including a special feature in the *Times Educational Supplement*. The school's own newsletter allowed staff and students to reflect on the highlights of the day and a key theme that emerged was the way it had brought people together to work as a team—staff alongside students.

> 'The main sponsor of the Environment Fair, Human Scale Education, places great emphasis on allowing young people to take responsibility for their education and we would like to think that the results of the students' hard work are a powerful indication of just what is possible when we hand over responsibility to them.'
> Settle High School newsletter, summer 2000

> 'Thank you for organising the Environment Fair. I thought my guide was very nice. I liked the treasure hunt best because it was quite hard and I liked the car engine as well. It hurt your knee a little bit as you crawled through! All the people were very kind and I liked it when we went in the leaf. Sometimes I had to bend down.' Olivia, primary school student

Looking back at the event seven years on, it is easy to view things through rose-tinted spectacles. Yet I can still remember the feeling of most observers that this was a ground-breaking event of real significance that should be shared with a wider audience. Nothing I've seen or read since then causes me to change this view. In fact the intervening years and my current professional distance from the school now allow me to judge things more objectively and only confirm my initial feelings that educational projects do not get much better than this. Clearly, some profound learning had taken place on that day in June.

A map for the millennium

Millennium year also provided the opportunity for people across the country to get involved in landmark projects that would enable them to remember this milestone for a lifetime. My department at Settle wanted to do something special that would allow us to provide a lasting record of our town in 2000. The idea of producing a special map of the town at this important point in its history seemed perfect, and so the Settle Millennium Map project was born. Now we just had to find some money to get the idea off the ground and convince the head that it would be okay to let the whole of year 9 loose on Settle during the winter months in order to have the map ready for unveiling in the summer!

Financial help came from the Royal Geographical Society who put us in touch with the Frederick Soddy Trust and their field study awards. Frederick Soddy was one of the UK'S foremost scientists researching radioactivity (receiving a Nobel Prize in chemistry in 1921) who later became interested in the study of society. Having had some experience of completing bids for funding, I was able to include the right phrases and buzzwords into our application. But more importantly, I understood the need to stress the innovative nature of the project and the central role that students would play. A few weeks after lodging the application in 1999 we received the good news that we'd been waiting for—we were to receive £450 in order to bring the project to fruition. My vision was that every student in year 9 would play a hands-on role in producing the map. In designing this project we obviously wanted to produce something of value to the community, but our reasons were not entirely altruistic—we were also keen to engender an interest in geography during the key decision year before GCSE option choices were made.

I was eager to involve the students in the plans for the map. I need to emphasise at this point that we were planning to produce much more than simply a *map* of the town. The completed map was to pick out detailed land use patterns, colour code every building according to use and would be surrounded by project work by the students which sought to cast light on the key features of Settle in 2000. I visited the feeder middle schools to outline our plans in the summer term of 1999, and was able to gain some valuable views on the information that could be collected from students who would join us in the autumn. This was fed back to the students via their teachers, so they could prepare themselves for the work to come. It was also used to design a leaflet about the project that was used to inform others about our work.

The funding from the Frederick Soddy Trust would pay for vital equipment needed for the project, the production of the launch leaflet and the printing of the finished map itself. We were expecting our students to be much more visible in the town when the fieldwork began in the autumn, and thankfully managed to get our leaflet sent out to every home in Settle inside the community newsletter which is delivered each month. This helped us to publicise our work, let residents know what were up to and also resulted in a fair bit of interest from people who offered help of various kinds.

> '*The community makes an effective contribution to students' learning. There are good links with the Settle Festival and a local art gallery. Students have the opportunity to be involved in local charitable initiatives and fundraising for the benefit of their school*'
>
> Ofsted report, January 2003

22 | We Did It Here!

The Settle Millennium Map

In addition to the work of the four geography teachers, there will be input into the project from staff in other departments at Settle High School & Community College. Look out for the following teachers in Settle with their Year 9 classes from September onwards.

Siân Doyle
Geography & PE teacher

Kathryn Needham
Geography & ICT teacher

Brinley Best
Geography Co-ordinator & ICT teacher

Keith Rodgers
Geography teacher & Duke of Edinburgh Scheme Co-ordinator

Request for help

From September 1999 onwards you will see students out and about in Settle carrying out their fieldwork. They may need to ask you a few questions or confirm how a building is used.

There are various other ways in which you can help with the project:

- Do you have any ideas about what you would like to see on the map? We would welcome the input of local people as we make our plans.
- We need to carry out more detailed interviews with residents, traders and business people in the town to learn about a typical day in their life – would you be willing to be interviewed?
- Are you a local 'expert' on any topic relating to the town? If so we want to hear from you.
- Would you like to sponsor the map? We are particularly interested to hear from local businesses who wish to have their logos printed on the map.
- Do you have map or computer skills, or equipment, which might help us produce our map, web site or CD-ROM?

We would be delighted to hear from you if you think you can help us with this exciting project, please contact:

Brinley Best (Geography Co-ordinator)
Settle High School & Community College
Settle
North Yorkshire
BD24 0AU
Telephone (01729) 822451
Fax (01729) 823830
e-mail gerg@nets.onyx.co.uk

Supported by Lamberts Press & Design, Settle, 01729 822177

A project organised by
Settle High School & Community College

Supported by
The Frederick Soddy Trust

We need your help! – read on for details

■ What is the Settle Millennium Map?

In September 1999 students at Settle High School & Community College will begin work on a special map of the town for publication in July 2000.

The aim of the project is to produce a snapshot of Settle at the turn of the 20th century through the medium of a Millennium Map. We also plan to produce a special Internet web site and a CD-ROM containing the results of the project.

This important project needs the help of people in Settle to make it a success – please read on to find out how you can assist in the production of the map.

■ What will be included in the map?

The map will contain a detailed record of how each building in Settle (including Giggleswick) is used. We will also look at the open spaces in and around the town and classify these too.

The large-format map will also contain other important information about the town and its people, including

- interviews with local traders and residents
- photographs of key sites
- reports on environmental issues affecting the town
- information from the most recent census

On completion of the project copies of the map will be placed in local libraries and will be widely available to local people as a lasting record of Settle at the turn of the Millennium.

■ How will the information be collected?

The map will be produced by 13 and 14-year-old students in their first year at Settle High School (Year 9), totalling over 150 students.

The town will be divided between each of the Year 9 classes and it will be their responsibility to collect the information required, with fieldwork being carried out in geography lessons.

The contents of the Millennium Map will be determined in consultation with the students themselves, and preliminary work has already taken place while they are still in Year 8 at Settle and Ingleton Middle Schools.

The students will be carrying out detailed land use surveys of the town, conducting interviews, carrying out traffic counts, completing field sketches and investigating environmental issues in small groups.

Back in the classroom the results will be written up by the students and produced in a form which can be included on the map, web site and CD-ROM. The final map will be the size of a large poster.

The Internet web site and CD-ROM will allow more detailed information to be presented than is possible on the map itself. We hope to include an in-depth profile of the town through these electronic media.

As well as providing a valuable resource and a lasting record of life in Settle at the turn of the century, the project will be of great educational value, developing a range of skills in the students. It will allow them to be involved in an innovative research project of significant value to the local community.

■ The team co-ordinating the project

The project will be co-ordinated by four teachers responsible for Year 9 geography teaching in the academic year 1999-2000 (see overleaf). They will be working with their classes on the fieldwork mainly in the autumn and spring terms (September 1999 to April 2000) as part of their National Curriculum work on the local area.

All the students in Year 9 will be involved in carrying out the fieldwork for the project and a smaller team of Year 9 students, aided by others in Years 10 to 13, will put together the web site and CD-ROM. This will take place as part of an Information and Communications Technology (ICT) club, which will benefit from the expertise of ICT teachers.

The publication of the results on the web site will occur throughout the project period as information becomes available. At the end of the project period the final map, web site and CD-ROM will be produced, and a report will be written outlining the achievements of the project.

■ A community project

We hope to involve the wider community in the project as much as possible and encourage you to contact us if you think you can help. A few suggestions of the ways in which you can help us are indicated overleaf.

We are grateful to the following for help with the project to date: Ann Carr, Peter Huby, Lamberts Newsagents, Lamberts Print and Design, Chris Leeming (Ingleton Middle School), Bill Mitchell MBE, Richard Warham (Settle Middle School), Settle Town Council.

A professionally printed leaflet was used to publicise the Settle Millennium Map

Once approval had been gained for the work from the head—who to his credit was happy to allow an extended period of fieldwork with its associated impact on other staff—all that remained was to divide up the town between the four geography teachers for the fieldwork phase. The students arrived in the autumn eager to begin work and their commitment and enthusiasm for the data collection was impressive. I had wanted to make sure that while a key focus was to produce the map, students should also be engaged in meaningful work of their own. So we devised an enquiry into tourism in Settle which each student would be required to write up, based on information they and their peers had collected. This was an important decision, as it reduced the chance that students would see the map exercise as an excuse to find a quiet corner of Settle in which to while away a lesson with their friends! As the project progressed we kept the community informed through regular updates in our school newsletter, via newspaper articles and on a special project website. The latter was an especially fine medium for posting photographs of students at work, and in due course, extracts from the draft map itself.

Students worked hard to complete their part of the map

24 | We Did It Here!

Students took great pride in their work on the Millennium Map

A smaller group of students completed the final version of the map

The map was unveiled at the Settle Community Festival

The fieldwork for the map was completed to schedule and a small group of dedicated students worked with us to create the map and associated material that would be unveiled at the launch event—the Settle Community Festival—which took place in June 2000. Our final thank you to the generous funder was to make a presentation, at their invitation, at the esteemed headquarters of the Royal Geographical Society in Kensington, London. It provided us with the opportunity to explain to a wider audience how the Settle Millennium Map had been put together, while also allowing us to showcase the success of the school on a national stage. The Frederick Soddy Trust were so pleased with the results of our work that they also asked us to write up the work for a geographical journal.

Youngsters win financial backing to survey the town for the millennium

School gets on the map

by **Bev Parkinson**

YOUNGSTERS at Settle High School hope to have the future of their town all mapped out by the end of this millennium.

In September the 13 and 14-year-olds will begin conducting land-use surveys, interviews and small-scale environmental projects to present a detailed picture of the town and its residents, as well as how they use the land, at the turn of the century.

A map will be designed in paper form and an electronic version, with extra information such as interviews, photographs and video footage, will also be created, to put on a special internet website and on CD-ROM.

The project can go ahead thanks to a grant from a trust established by Nobel prize-winning scientist Professor Frederick Soddy.

Fieldwork

The trust aims to encourage students to engage more actively in fieldwork projects with direct relevance to local communities.

The school's map project was one of only seven projects nationally to be awarded a grant.

Geography students at Settle High School, from left, Sue Kilburn, Rowan Pickles, Katie Birkett and Lesley Collier preparing for the Millennium Map project. 110599-9.

Press releases to local newspapers ensured a high media profile for the Millennium Map project Image reproduced with permission of the Lancaster Guardian

Bringing Settle together

> *'Wouldn't it be great if we could produce a large print version of our school newsletter for older people who live locally?'* John Smith, year 9 student

Such helpful and insightful comments by students were a pretty standard feature of life at Settle High School. Yet no one could have guessed where this astute observation from a year 9 student would have taken the school. And no one could have imagined that it would result in the winning of a high profile national award and the school gaining headlines in broadsheet newspapers. The Settle *Together!* Project, born out of John Smith's suggestion, achieved just that. But it achieved much more besides—it helped to establish the school as a provider of vital services to the community, and even resulted in a wedding!

> *'Students eagerly offer help both in the school and the local community'*
>
> Ofsted report, January 2003

One of the challenges of living in an attractive rural community such as Settle is that, for demographic reasons, there is a danger of polarisation. The region attracts more than its fair share of retired people which, added to the indigenous community of older people, results in an age structure skewed in favour of the mature years. The presence of several thriving schools in the town, with a cohort of children in excess of a thousand, means that there's the potential for the divide and tensions between young and old to be acute. Young people can be dismissive of older folk, viewing them stereotypically; older people can be suspicious of the young and their unfamiliar ways. So it seemed that the well-meant suggestion of producing a large print newsletter to inform older people about what was happening at the school could go some way to bridging that gap—even though a good number of the retirees in Settle still have perfectly good eyesight!

We hit upon the idea of organising a major project that would see a whole range of events, workshops and activities that would encourage the sharing of skills and knowledge in Settle. The spirit of the activities was that young and older people could come together in order to work in harmony—with benefits for all. Central to our aims as a school, we also wished to ensure that students would play their full part in the project through their work on a student management team that made all the key decisions.

An important feature of the project from the start was the involvement of the local branch of Age Concern, a national charity working to promote the well-being of older people. We found a key ally in Sue Mann, the chief officer in Settle, who understood straight away what we wanted to achieve and committed time and resources to the project. She also agreed to serve on the management team that would steer the project towards its launch, a team that also included staff from the school, a governor, a local community representative and—vitally—students. There's a sense of camaraderie that comes from working within a cohesive team that makes one feel that anything is possible. Inspired by a shared vision we had several very productive meetings after school and put together a very strong and ambitious bid which found an ideal funder in the form of the Barclays New Futures Award for citizenship. This high profile national scheme was a leading funder of innovative projects in schools in the late 1990s and early 2000s. The scheme provided the project with a generous budget of £7,000 for two years of work, but we had big plans and wanted to extend activities into a third year—cue Booths Supermarkets, our community partner, who had just opened a store in the town and wanted to cement links with the community. This family-owned supermarket group generously provided an additional £6,000 that enabled the project to have a wider impact, as well as being extended into a third year.

To get the project off with a bang a high profile launch evening was scheduled, which also had the aim of seeking the views of local people on the activities to be included in the project. So it was that 100 people gathered at Settle's Victoria Hall in June 2001 in order to celebrate the beginning of the Settle *Together!* Project. The evening was given an added frisson of excitement by the presence of celebrated actress Thelma Barlow, a local resident, who had agreed to be the project patron. Thelma even helped to set the ball rolling by offering to lead organic gardening classes—a particular passion of hers. One of my favourite suggestions that came out of the launch evening was an abseiling course—suggested by a 65-year-old grandmother who had recently had a hip replacement!

Settle Together! timetable of events

Autumn 2000

- Bid submitted and funding from Barclays and Booths Supermarkets secured.

Spring 2001

- Detailed planning for project.

Summer 2001

- Late June—launch party with Thelma Barlow (canvassing of ideas with audience).

Autumn 2001

- Gala performance of *The Snow Queen*—mixed audience of students from all schools, older family members and Age Concern clients.
- Quiz afternoon and tea—teams from businesses and families.
- A variety of workshops to develop skills.

Spring 2002

- Balloon-building challenge and lunch—mixed-age teams worked to build tissue paper balloons in a race against the clock to see who could create a structure that flew.

Summer 2002

- Shopping trip to Trafford Centre—meanwhile students took part in presentation in Manchester as part of CSV/Barclays evaluation programme.

Autumn 2002

- Trip to Blackpool Illuminations (approximately eighty participants of all ages)—quiz on journey to encourage discussion.

Spring 2003

- Craft day—120 participants took part in a range of craft activities, including felt making, paper making, bookbinding and Chinese calligraphy.

Summer 2003

- Technology day—information and opportunity to learn more about a range of household gadgets, computers, internet and broadband.
- Question and answer sessions on computer troubleshooting.
- Mystery trip to coincide with Father's Day—games and quiz on bus to reveal final destination (Chester and Stapley Water Gardens).

Autumn 2003

- Second trip to Blackpool Illuminations—ninety-six participants this time! Usual quiz and games on bus.

- Trip to Edinburgh with guided bus tour and opportunity to visit Britannia (maps and information packs provided as well as Edinburgh observation quiz).

Spring 2004

- Theatre trip to *Wind in The Willows* at West Yorkshire Playhouse Millennium Archive day—a chance for local groups to make posters to give information about their organisation's activities since 2000 as part of display in the town hall.

Summer 2004

- The finale—a trip to London with time for shopping, a choice of three top shows, private pods on the Millennium Wheel and overnight stay (maps and information packs provided).

Autumn 2004

- An extra—a trip to Edinburgh for Christmas market with ghost walk in the evening and overnight stay before visiting Glasgow (maps and information packs provided).

Two students' views on the Settle Together! project

John Smith

'The management and co-ordination were an incredibly educational and motivating experience, and the conference in Manchester was excellent. Settle Together! strengthened my relationship with some companies that we used to supply us with goods and services, and also has helped me understand the complexities of running such a huge project with national recognition.'

John Smith was the student whose idea initiated the project and led the organisation of the final trip to London.

Amy Preston

> 'I feel Settle Together! brought me out of my shell and made me a more confident person around others. I feel my skills as a person have improved. My favourite adventure with my team was going to London; how I ever managed to lead a group through London late at night I will never know. I can't stop telling people about the project, it was a fantastic opportunity to be able to work with a team.'

Amy Preston was a year 10 student when the project began and took on important responsibilities for running aspects of the project from the outset.

The project was very warmly received by the community and people quickly signed up for activities and trips. These included a community choir, balloon making workshops, quiz events, a technology day run by students for older people, a trip to the Blackpool Illuminations and a gala performance of the musical *The Snow Queen*, staged for primary school children who had to bring a relative over 55 years old with them. The events certainly achieved their aim of bringing people closer together—much more so than was expected. Two local residents, brought together by a shared passion for Scotland, signed up for a cultural visit to Edinburgh during the height of the project and a year later were married!

'The school has successfully developed very good links with the community'

Ofsted report, January 2003

The Settle *Together!* Project is remembered fondly by students, staff and residents of Settle, and played an important role in helping the school to be seen as the focus of the community and the generator of high quality educational projects. These were projects which valued lifelong learning as much as the needs of the students in Settle's schools.

The team also produced the planned large print edition of a Settle *Together!* newsletter which was sponsored by Magna Books, a large print book publisher based locally. A website, designed and maintained by students, was also launched.

The project has provided a lasting legacy for several of the participating students. John Smith, whose idea for a large print newsletter first gave birth to Settle *Together!*, is currently a key worker for the charity Age Concern in Settle, providing and servicing all their office technology. Another student who worked on the school's newsletter is now a key member of the editorial team producing the popular Settle Community News.

Communicating the message

At an early stage the school recognised that communication tools would play a significant role in maximising its community work. Perhaps most important, a comprehensive newsletter was identified as a key vehicle for promoting community activities and encouraging local people to get involved. The decision was taken in 1995 to launch a half-termly newsletter, edited by a member of staff, which would be produced in-house and distributed to all students and the wider community. The transition from a simple word-processed document on its launch in 1995 to a professional desk-top published newsletter by the year 2000 was impressive. It also signalled the seriousness with which the school viewed its communications work.

Staff and students were encouraged to contribute both news and features, and slowly a production team—comprising chiefly students—was assembled to ease the burden on the editor. It soon became clear that the newsletter could also bring a range of other benefits to the school. It provided an important platform for students' journalistic skills to be developed and gave a small group the opportunity to develop team-working capability in a real life environment. The discipline of regular deadlines helped to focus students' minds and encouraged them to become more skilled at managing their time. It also allowed young people to showcase their work across a range of subject areas, within and outside the main curriculum, including photography, art and poetry. Innovative features such as interviews with well-known local residents, students' book and record reviews, puzzle pages, a student recipe slot and a 'creative corner' of students' work were introduced, all aimed at engaging readers and demonstrating the breadth of work taking place at the school.

A high quality school magazine helped Settle High School & Community College to promote its achievements

news@settle.high production team

Production team

Editor	Brin Best
Assistant Editor	John Weir
News Editor	Lindsay Longbottom 13LH
Sports Editor	Sally Shepherd 13BB
Year 9 Reporters	Amy Sanderson 9SD, Corrine Redfern 9SD, Anna Wilding 9NP, Claire Atherton 9NP, Lucy Ammundsen 9JW
Year 10 reporters	Vicky Pinner 10RN, Stephen Whitfield 10SP, Alison Thornton 10SP
Year 11 reporters	Wayne Hudson 11MT, Chris Woodcock 11TM
Year 12 reporter	Shona Matthew 12BB
Year 13 reporters	Charlotte Taylor 13CW, Sophie Mascoll 13MH, Sarah Hutchinson 13MH
Computer reporter	Amy Preston 10FH
Puzzles	Sam Chan 11TM
Features Editor	John Smith 10SP
Art Editor	Rosie Palmer 13BB
Artist	Michelle Robinson 10SP
Reviews Editor	Cheryl Ford 12PE
Reviewers	Nick Parker 10RN
Picture Editor	Keiran Hunt 9KN
Photographer	Sally Shillito
Proof-reader	Peter Metcalfe

Thanks to the following contributors to this issue

Gill O'Donnell
Lionel Edwards
Helen Fish
Jennifer Iball
Laura Richardson
Katherine Round
Beci Shepherd

Printed by Lamberts Print & Design
01729 822177

This year's publication dates

Autumn	October 20
Christmas	December 20
Winter	February 16
Spring	April 6
Whitsun	May 25
Summer	July 20

The magazine production team was mainly drawn from the student population

A different colour paper was chosen for each issue and the newsletter was printed on the school's risograph machine for about ten pence per unit. On the day of issue, the school was awash with colour as students eagerly thumbed through the newsletter—it was genuinely appreciated by the youngsters as much as the staff. Copies were also distributed widely in the community, to feeder primary schools, libraries, post offices and tourist information centres—indeed anywhere where people might gather who could be interested in what was happening at the school. Many positive comments were received from members of the public and it was clear that the reputation of the school had been enhanced by this simple measure.

A key figure during this period was our new head of ICT, Roger Davies, a person who in another role will figure prominently in the next chapter. Roger breathed new life into the newsletter through his imaginative design ideas. He also taught us that to appeal to younger readers it was perfectly valid for us to take lessons from the designers of our popular tabloid newspapers. The result was that the appearance of the publication changed from being rather staid and formal to something much more inviting for readers of all ages. Through his enthusiasm, good humour and hard work, Roger also helped to establish the newsletter as a key part of community life for the school and the wider community. During his year working with us, the editorial team behind the newsletter grew substantially, most notably in terms of the number of student members contributing material.

Such initiatives sometimes have unexpected results. Some of the student production team were so inspired by their taste of journalism that they chose to study the subject at college or university, and at least one of them is currently being groomed for a high profile role as a sports writer for a national newspaper. He freely admits that being sports editor of Settle High School's newsletter helped him to learn the ropes and discipline of journalism. It clearly helped to ignite his inner fire for writing that has remained with him to this day.

The newsletter admirably achieved its aim of providing a platform to publicise the community work of the school. When the decision was taken to start designing and printing it professionally, in a revamped glossy magazine-style format, local businesses were eager to offer their support by paying for advertising. This enabled the newsletter to effectively pay for itself and the more professional feel of the finished product brought the school additional credit.

A newsletter can only achieve so much, so the school ensured that its communications strategy extended far beyond a half-termly periodical that, despite its success, some local people may not read regularly. The role of public relations officer was created, a post which initially went to an enthusiastic teacher who was given a little time off from teaching to liaise with the media to ensure the widest possible coverage for the school. The issuing of professional press releases was a vital development during this period. Every week at least one press release went to local and regional newspapers and the result was a steady flow of positive stories about the school, together with frequent phone calls from journalists and editors actually *asking* for stories. Local radio too was utilised and following a course on managing the media, the PR officer undertook regular radio interviews about the school. These proved especially useful when the school wanted to announce a new event or activity, or ask for local participation in a project.

As the amount of news being fed to the PR officer increased, and the importance and possibilities of the post became clear, the role transferred to a non-teaching member of support staff who could more easily telephone journalists and arrange photo shoots during the school day. Some major PR successes occurred during this period, not least full page articles in the national tabloid newspapers—and a high profile Sky News TV feature—about a student who had never missed a day off school in his life. This resulted in positive publicity about the school that would have costs tens of thousands of pounds. Records of all media coverage were kept on file and newspaper cuttings were displayed prominently on a 'celebration board' which greeted visitors on entry.

The 'secrets' of success

In the first part of this chapter I've tried to offer a flavour of what it was like—from the perspective of a participant—to witness Settle High School's efforts to draw even closer to its community. There were many other events and projects during this period of a similar magnitude to those described above, which there's no room for here to document fully. It was certainly a very special period in the school's history and I feel privileged to have been part of it. But as this book is about trying to document *how* schools have achieved success as much as it is concerned with *what* they have done, I now wish to reflect on what the key factors were that led to success in this beautiful part of Yorkshire. Ten factors stand out in terms of their importance.

Creative approaches

Incredibly powerful things can happen when a body of staff is united by a passion for a particular approach to learning. And their efforts are given greater magnitude when those that matter—senior leaders and governors—encourage and nurture this passion. A strong tradition of performing arts at the school, most notably drama, had infused the institution with an ethos where creativity, in all its forms, was seen as a key force binding staff together. But perhaps more significantly, previous success in using creative approaches had encouraged teachers to innovate and try out unconventional approaches and, critically, the headteacher and governors had given their vociferous approval of such efforts. The result was that the school's community work during the critical period was injected with a sense of imagination that immediately appealed to those it was seeking to embrace.

'Thinking big'

One of the important lessons gained from the work of Settle High School and Community College is that if you think big amazing things are possible. Not content just to organise easily manageable, small scale projects the school took bold steps into the unknown by organising complex events and activities—projects that stood a much better chance of having a real lasting impact on the community. This willingness to think big also brought the school considerable media attention and this helped to build the profile of the school still further.

Real life learning opportunities

Learning is surely most powerful when it has real relevance to students' lives and the world outside school. Many of the projects that the school organised had a distinctive flavour of authenticity—from the running of decision-making committees by students to the production of newsletter articles for their peers that had to engage if they were not to be ignored. The feedback of many of the students participating in the projects highlighted the benefits they had gained that took them beyond the realms of the National Curriculum into genuine lifelong learning. The school had clearly managed to extend its educational offering some years before the notion of 'Extended Schools' became fashionable. The way in which students so readily engaged with challenges that staff threw at them spoke volumes about the success of the projects being organised, and was clearly a key factor that enabled the school to pull them off so effectively.

Careful planning

The phrase 'poor planning prevents high performance' is drummed into teachers at an early stage in their careers as they struggle to design lessons that inspire learners. Yet when it comes to planning projects, this familiar phrase is sometimes forgotten. One of the key hallmarks of the work of the school was a meticulous approach to planning. For example, the Environment Fair required a management team of staff who met on a monthly basis. These meetings were given high profile by being held in a local pub after school ended, with the added bonus of a tasty buffet to keep staff energy levels up. The spirit of teamwork meant that every person attending left with a series of action points that they were fully committed to carrying through in the agreed timescale. Another example was the drafting process for the funding application for the Settle *Together!* Project. The team behind this project, which included two students as well as staff, governors and community representatives, met to draft out the application and came together again to review further drafts as the scale of the project became clear. The team's willingness to plan the project so carefully made a very significant difference to the overall quality of the bid, which was judged as one of the most effective the Barclays New Futures team had ever come across.

Time found for things that were important

Schools are busy places and for some teachers it seems like there's never enough time to cope with the status quo, never mind take on additional work. Yet staff at Settle High School and Community College challenged this notion and made a concerted effort to *make* time for those things they most valued. The results were very powerful. Many staff actually felt energised by the process and found new reserves of creativity. Others went on record to say how the projects they had been involved in had helped to renew their enthusiasm for teaching, or helped them to see the community in a new light. There was a tangible feeling that staff were steering the school towards a more exciting future, and the projects were adding value to what they did on a day to day basis in the classroom. Significantly, they were also helping to enhance relationships with their students and key figures in the community.

Successes promoted— leading to further success

It certainly pays to promote your successes. Settle High School and Community College is a superb example of a school where success has bred further success. One example is the Settle *Together!* Project, which began as a two year initiative attracting funding of £7,000 but quickly caught the attention of a supermarket chain, which added a further £6,000 to the pot. This enabled the project to widen its scope and span for a further year. The sponsors were impressed by the imaginative nature of the project, and called on the school to attend promotional events. They even featured the school in a broadsheet newspaper article about the programme. All this gave the school an opportunity to raise its profile, make some friends in high places and generally help to raise aspirations for staff, students and parents. When, a few years later, the school came to apply for specialist technology status, it was able to rein in favours and appeal to those who had helped previously. A cheque for £5,000 soon arrived from the supermarket chain, and the rest of the funds followed on from that.

Issues of local importance

The school never forgot that its main purpose was to serve the needs of its local population. True to this vision it selected very carefully projects that people could see had a clear link to local issues—issues that were prominent in the minds of people who lived and worked in the hinterland of Settle. As such, the Environment Fair had a very rural flavour, with local farmers lending animals and equipment for the day; the Settle *Together!* Project tackled issues that had been recognised in the community plan; the Millennium Map project tapped into a pride in the long history of the town. By engaging the interest of local people and groups, they were galvanised to offer support and a powerful resource base was assembled.

Collaboration with local groups and people

Many schools give lip service to the notion of collaboration, but Settle High School and Community College went to great lengths to ensure that there were genuine links with the community. A good example is the role of Age Concern in the Settle *Together!* Project. A member of staff who saw the potential for this charity to work with the school organised an exploratory meeting with their local chief officer to explore the common ground. Rapidly, a shared passion to bridge the generation divide was recognised, which ultimately resulted in Age Concern being the major community partner for the three year intergenerational project that is described in detail earlier.

Staff committed to going that extra mile

High quality projects can only happen if there are people working their socks off behind the scenes to make them a reality. There's no doubt that during the period described the majority of staff at the school were willing to put in *considerable* time and energy to set up inspirational projects. It is important to place on record here the fact that, although serving a rural catchment area which was to some extent insulated from some of the pressures affecting schools in urban settings, the school had its fair share of challenges and difficulties. This was far from an educational utopia.

Students empowered to play their part

There was a sense of student ownership of the projects described that is hard to put into words, but is immediately apparent to those who witnessed them. Some of the testimonies from students included above hint at how this ownership manifested itself. Such student engagement only happens when staff are prepared to open up, take risks and hand over in a genuine way the management of projects to students. The fact that young people were queuing up to run events that they had devised for the Environment Day is testament to the culture of student empowerment at the school. This extended far beyond just involving the most able or willing—some of the most successful participants in the activities described were those students who found their own unique but high impact way to take part. These were often not those youngsters who excelled in the classroom. There are surely important lessons here for all of us engaged in finding ways of motivating learners.

> 'Students have been very involved with the community suggesting, for example, the environmental improvements they would like for Settle'
>
> Ofsted report, January 2003

How transferable is this work?

I want to end this chapter—as I will do with those that follow—by considering how much other schools might benefit from the work showcased here; how many common principles there might be that are transferable. The key question is, to what extent can other schools mirror what has been done and achieve similar success in their own settings? This is a critical issue, as it gets to the heart of success in schools by focusing on the factors that can bring schools closer to their goals.

I think it is clear from the 'secrets of success' section that there is much that other schools *can* do to model the ethos, outlook and actions of Settle High School and Community College. There seems nothing unique here that other teachers and leaders cannot strive for in their own schools. Clearly, though, key leaders at the school had recognised the potential of staff and given them crucial licence to think big and innovate—something which is not always built into the ethos of every school. They also were prepared to commit resources to the things that mattered to the school, much as staff committed their time to bring projects to fruition.

A key question that will resurface time and time again in the book is the extent to which successful schools rely on driven, creative *individuals* to make changes happen: people who are full of ideas, energy and enthusiasm, who brim with confidence and who never give up until they get what they want. While I'd like to think that your school is currently full of such people, they do tend to be thin on the ground, yet we have all probably seen how they can transform schools. They are inspirational individuals.

My belief is that the work of Settle High School and Community College benefited from some of these key people—let's call them 'drivers'—but that other staff, some with less innate drive and passion, also played important but less high profile roles. While 'drivers' are clearly important in providing leadership in every school, they're also important role models—people whose actions and attitudes we can try to model if we want to develop as individuals. This is illustrated by the fact that some of the staff who took a lesser role in the projects described are now at the forefront of projects happening in new schools they have joined.

We are surely not fixed with the knowledge, skills and dispositions that we possess when we begin working at a school. To think so would be to undermine one of the central tenets of education—that we are lifelong learners. As in any profession, we all begin as apprentices and need to look for people that inspire us in order to stretch ourselves and develop. The 'secrets of success' can, therefore, be seen as success factors; things that can be modelled if we wish to develop our abilities and become more successful in our own schools. But any such development will only happen if we *believe* in ourselves, if we believe we can change, gain new skills and gain fresh perspectives. The role of our senior leaders in giving us the confidence to do this is paramount, and is a theme we will come back to later in the book.

This story of success in a Yorkshire school is uplifting—and it has already inspired several other schools to try out similar approaches as they strive to draw closer to their communities. But in one case study it was not possible to judge objectively the full range of factors underpinning successful schools. Some wider research and further stories and testimonies from additional schools would be needed for a more objective evidence base to be assembled. Finally, the path my journey would need to follow began to take shape. The remainder of this book is an account of the journey to uncover these schools, which has taken me from my home in Yorkshire throughout England in search of education excellence. My first port of call lay a few miles over the county border in Cumbria, where I had heard that spectacular results were being achieved with information and communications technology.

> *'The school continues to be an exceptionally harmonious community'*
>
> Ofsted report, January 2003

Chapter 2

Scholarship and Care in the Shadow of the Fells

> *'It's always intriguing to speculate on what makes a school successful and indeed it is not too difficult to identify the characteristics that good places seem to have in common. But when it comes down to it, it takes very special people to make these elements cohere and coalesce.'* Chris Clarke, headteacher, Queen Elizabeth School, Kirkby Lonsdale

While some schools have a buzz that is tangible as soon as you enter the building, a few manage to be so lively in everything they do that the place positively vibrates. Such was the feeling that overwhelmed me the first time I set foot inside Queen Elizabeth School (QES) in Kirkby Lonsdale. My contact at the school was a former colleague from Settle, Roger Davies, who had accepted the post of director of ICT at QES in 1999. A Yorkshireman by birth, Roger had spent seven years in the printing industry before joining the teaching profession as a mature teacher in 1991. His move to Cumbria followed time spent learning the craft of ICT leadership in a tough comprehensive school in inner London and a rural school over the county border in Yorkshire. Always passionate about the role of IT in education, Roger has been involved in this aspect of schools for all his sixteen years in the job. When I met him on a blustery January day, Roger appeared as youthful as I'd remembered him from our days together editing Settle High School's newsletter.

I had driven past QES many times on my trips to and from the Lake District and Lancashire coast: it is situated within clear sight of the

A65 trunk road that during holiday time is humming with traffic. The school nestles between the western Yorkshire Dales to the east and the first of the Cumbrian fells to the north. Though apparently serving a very rural catchment area—Kirkby Lonsdale is a smart market town within a farming community—Lancastrian coastal conurbations lie only a few miles to the west. In recent years the school has accepted more and more youngsters from these areas, giving it a very diverse student population and an increase in numbers on the roll from 650 fifteen years ago to the current total of over 1,380. In line with this growth the school has undergone a major building programme in the past few years, almost doubling the amount of space the school occupies.

Creating something special

In collaboration with Mark McNulty, the school's director of e-learning who joined the school in 1999 as a newly qualified teacher, Roger Davies has built something truly special at QES. These technological wizards have, through the wonderfully creative use of hardware and software, helped to embed ICT as a central plank in the school's efforts to engage and inspire learners. The evidence is there to see in every nook and cranny of this labyrinth of a school, whose oldest buildings date back to 1591. The school has no less than 430 computers available for student use, with the aspiration that in time this 1,384-strong school will have enough computers so that no student ever has to share facilities when they need access to ICT. Barring those classrooms where it is not currently appropriate, every conceivable space has been turned into a computer suite or cluster, or is earmarked for development. Linking these machines is an intricate backbone of cabling, installed by a local IT company, which Roger and his team have designed to be expandable as the need arises. In doing so, Roger has tackled the first of the four key challenges he identified when joining the school—the *technical challenge* to provide a robust and scaleable infrastructure (see diagram opposite).

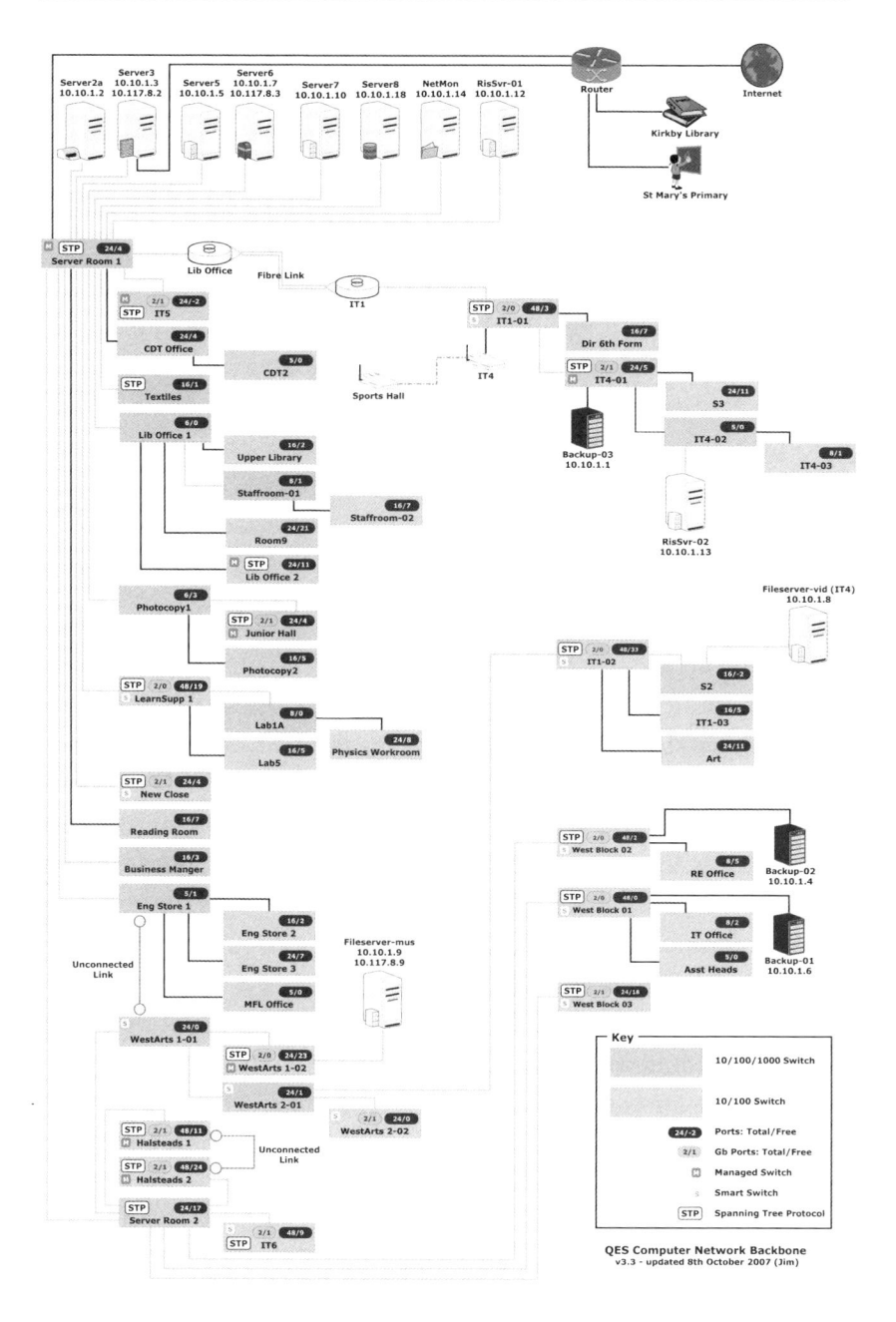

Chapter 2: Scholarship and Care in the Shadow of the Fells

ICT infrastructure at Queen Elizabeth School

Four challenges to developing ICT in schools

These challenges were conceived by Roger Davies and form the core of the work undertaken by QES to embed ICT into the curriculum and to inspire learners at all key stages.

1. *The technical challenge*: providing a robust and scaleable infrastructure.
2. *The pupil challenge*: providing a coherent programme of study to develop students' ICT capability.
3. *The teaching challenge*: empowering teachers in all subjects to embrace the creative potential offered by ICT.
4. *The management challenge*: utilising the integrated network to streamline administration and provide data focused on student attainment.

The school's current high quality ICT provision seems a different world to the state of affairs when Roger joined the school in 1999. Alarmed by the virtual absence of ICT facilities at that time, Roger set out in a rented truck to claim eighty dilapidated PCs from his former school in inner London which were destined for a landfill site. Over the summer holiday prior to his first term at the school, Roger built QES's first computer network, breathing new life into equipment that seemed beyond repair. By the time the fresh-faced year 7s were arriving for their induction day, thirty computers were awaiting them.

> 'An outstanding school which gives excellent value for money'
>
> *Ofsted report, October 2005*

Roger's hands-on approach is something that marks him out as a person who is happy to get stuck in and make things happen on the ground—but he is also comfortable leading high level whole-school training sessions on the use of ICT. Together with Mark, also a late entrant to teaching following many years in publishing, they make a formidable team leading ICT across the school. Their work is now supported by an expanded ICT department that includes a recently appointed head of ICT, three further specialist ICT teachers and no fewer than five full-time ICT technicians. It would be hard to find a more dedicated or skilled group of educationalists, united by their passion for the value of ICT to enhance learning.

Roger's mission when taking over as ICT coordinator focused on the four challenges he identified shortly after coming into post—the technical, pupil, teaching and management challenges. But underpinning all his work was also a belief that he must work towards three more specific goals—goals that would ultimately help him and others to judge that ICT was beginning to have a major impact on the school (see box below). Hand in hand with the achievement of these goals there has clearly also been a culture change in the use of ICT across the school over the last six years, which has been made possible by the rapid development of the state-of-the-art technical infrastructure that underpins it all. Teachers no longer see ICT as something that students do in specific lessons using equipment only familiar to specialists; instead it is increasingly recognised as a tool to enhance learning across the curriculum, *within* subject lessons.

Three ICT goals for QES

- Every teacher should have their own laptop.
- When working on computer during a lesson, every student should be able to use their own machine.
- There should be a data projector in every classroom.

> 'A key point about the infrastructure is the fact that, if you want staff to embed it in practice it has to work. Everyone knows IT will go wrong at some time—just as light bulbs blow—but having a large on-site technical team means that when it does, it gets fixed—and fast! This, to me, is the major technical achievement—the provision of a helpful support service that staff can rely on.' Roger Davies

ICT developments at QES 1999–2007

Dates	Technical challenge	Pupil challenge
1999–2000	Provide enough computers to teach IT lessons as timetabled. Done through rebuilding from parts by Aug 1999. *Feb 2000*: install three new machines and server to provide internet access in library. *Easter 2000*: roll out fledgling whole school network to equip two rooms with computers for IT teaching. *Summer 2000*: equip third room with networked PCs. Install cable backbone with minimum of one network point in every room thus allowing network to scale up.	Draft a scheme of work for Key Stage 3. Implement changes to GCSE and A-level syllabus taught.

Teaching/learning challenge	*Management challenge*
Introduce IT Development Group meeting half-termly.	Not a priority at this stage.
Introduce termly staff newsletter about ICT developments.	
Conduct staff IT audit.	
Inset sessions arranged to introduce utility to produce reports from statement banks.	

ICT developments at QES 1999–2007 continued

Dates	Technical challenge	Pupil challenge
2000–2001	*Sept 2000*: install fledgling intranet, install mail server and give all staff e-mail addresses. *Nov 2000*: employ full time IT technician. *Sept 2000*: all departmental offices equipped with networked PCs. *Christmas 2000*: clusters of PCs put in learning support area, library, art and business studies departments. *Summer 2001*: further clusters in food technology and Upper Library.	*Sept 2000*: introduce discrete ICT for one hour per week for all at Key Stage 3. Development of Key Stage 3 scheme of work made available across intranet. Experiment with self marking web-based tests.

Teaching/learning challenge	Management challenge
Oct 2000: inset sessions on file management on a network and e-mail.	Sept 2000: develop IT room booking system.
Sept 2000: create e-team (pupils who produce content for intranet).	Throughout year: make as many 'admin' templates, proformas, etc. as possible available on school network (for staff only).
Nov 2000: organise first cohort of NOF (New Opportunities Funding) training. School website (first version) goes live, created by two pupils.	
Throughout year: regular drop-in sessions for any staff after school on Thursdays.	
Two Sony Mavica cameras proving very popular!	
Jan 2001: first digital projector purchased. Inset sessions on PowerPoint and using projector.	
June 2001: inset sessions on Publisher (desktop publishing software).	

ICT developments at QES 1999–2007 *continued*

Dates	Technical challenge	Pupil challenge
2002–2003	Servers upgraded. Further clusters of networked PCs in science area. *Jan 2003*: experimental clusters of wireless laptops in D & T and history introduced.	First lessons in basic video editing. Introduction of AVCE ICT to run alongside computing at AS-level.

Teaching/learning challenge	*Management challenge*
Jan 2003: two full days IT inset for all staff arranged and delivered by IT staff. *Mar 2003*: all staff completed NOF training. *Sept 2002*: inset sessions on developing intranet content for departments. Mark works with departments to develop intranet/web-based content in English, PSHE, science, geography and RE. First e-learning credits spent, with allocation through IT Development Group.	Distribute 'Teachers Toolkit', a set of templates developed to help with all departmental admin. (e.g. standard markbooks, detention reminders, etc.). Organise inset sessions to support Toolkit, aimed at heads of department.

ICT developments at QES 1999–2007 continued

Dates	Technical challenge	Pupil challenge
2003– 2004	Expansion means network now supports 300+ PCs. *Sept 2003:* reorganisation of shared areas/folders on school network. Strain on technicians evident, begin to establish procedures for fault reporting and help. *Feb 2004:* develop online fault reporting system. Technical staff enrolled on modular training, leading to system admin degrees.	First cohort of school piloting QCA online test. *Jan 2004:* Mark shortlisted for TES (Times Educational Supplement) ICT In Practice Awards.
2004– 2005	*Summer 2004:* New sixth form library equipped. Further expansion towards A Laptop for Every Teacher (achieved), A Computer for Every Child (all whole class suites expanded to thirty machines), a projector for every room (planned rollout through year). Network now 400 PCs including video editing and music suites. *Apr 2005:* two more technicians employed. Remote Access to school network provided via CLEO. *July 2005:* junior technician added to team.	Double award Applied ICT GCSE started.

Teaching/learning challenge	Management challenge
Sept 2003: 'Back to Basics' series of inset sessions aimed at less confident staff.	Admin. network integrated into whole school network and office re-equipped with new PCs.
Begin working with Cumbria Pathfinder on e-learning initiatives.	All remaining staff issued with laptops.
Trial SAM Learning and Scholar.	
May 2005: start trialling Moodle VLE.	Ten inset sessions on 'Encouraging use of ICT' for departmental inset (key concepts).
	SIMS upgraded and made more widely available for staff.
	Address Cumbria headteachers on Framework for ICT Technical Support.
	Develop whole school reporting system.

ICT developments at QES 1999–2007 continued

Dates	Technical challenge	Pupil challenge
2005–2006	Further expansion to around 500 PCs. Start of rolling replacement strategy. Roll out remote network access to staff. Restructure IT support around model recomended in FITS (Flexible Image Transport System). Progressive development of FITS help desk model.	Begin transfer and reworking of material from intranet to Moodle for all ICT courses.
2006–2007	Relocate help desk to separate fault reporting from fault resolution. Begin investigating virtualisation for servers. Set up virtual test bed.	Moodle becomes consolidated in wide variety of subjects. School's Moodle development features on Teachers' TV.

Teaching/learning challenge	Management challenge
Development of Moodle and inset for staff throughout year.	Creation of Data Management Group bringing together stakeholders to drive development of admin. software.

Development in use of timetabling, exams, admin. software.

Expansion of school admin. team.

Begin consolidation of prior assessment data. |
| Further development of courseware in Moodle. Particular focus on social software side, such as discussion forums. | Begin installation of electronic registration.

Develop procedures for logging behavioural incidents electronically. |

Major breakthroughs

As I discussed the ICT revolutions that have take place at QES since Roger joined the school, his eyes lit up at particular moments as he remembered key milestones along the way. Looking back, these can be seen as significant breakthroughs that have had a profound influence on the use of ICT at the school.

Perhaps the most notable ICT development over the last few years has been the introduction of the school's Virtual Learning Environment (VLE). In short, this allows subject resources, web-links, quizzes, communication and collaboration tools such as forums, assignments for comment and 'wikis' (shared editable documents) all to be stored online and thus be accessible anytime, anywhere. Following extensive trials organised through the local authority, the school chose Moodle as the basis for its own VLE and Mark's expertise in this aspect of ICT has enabled the school to become a leader in the use of such platforms to enhance learning. The use of VLEs also addressed one of the school's past mistakes of trying to turn teachers into webmasters. For several years the school had built a comprehensive intranet—this was a vital stepping stone on the learning journey—but ordinary staff couldn't get to grips with adding content. Moodle makes things much easier.

The advent of free but high quality software is also making an important difference to the quality of learning at QES. Suitable programs are identified by staff and uploaded to the VLE. Examples in use during my visit included the mapping program Google Earth (essentially a Geographical Information System), the music editing software Audacity, GameMaker and Scratch (wonderful programs to teach computer programming in a fun engaging way) and the 3-D design program Google Sketch-up. Subject teachers take responsibility for finding ways of integrating such programs into lessons, sometimes supported by specialist input from ICT staff. Although there is a specific pedagogy linked to the use of such tools, it is vital for subject teachers to teach the skills in the context of specific subject areas; this is supported by discrete ICT lessons at Key Stage 3.

> 'The provision of discrete ICT lessons throughout Key Stage 3 means staff are freed from the chore of teaching the basic skills—we do it, and staff can make educational use of the software without getting bogged down in how to teach students how to use it—students know that already from their ICT lessons.'
> Roger Davies

Roger identified the effective use of email correspondence as another key breakthrough for the school. This has not only allowed staff to communicate more easily among themselves, but perhaps more significantly, has opened up lines of communication with students. Staff can be emailed with homework, queries or updates by students and emails are used in a multitude of ways to enhance learning opportunities in the school. In my later conversations with students at the school, individuals spoke passionately about the positive effects of email facilities, especially the ability to log on to the school email system at home. Remote access is gathering pace, with staff now able to access a school computer from home if they wish, actually running programs, sending work to school printers and so on. The school is now implementing plans for students to access files stored at school from home. This is cutting-edge provision and was part of Roger's development plan back in 2000.

> 'Relationships between pupils and teachers are excellent and contribute to the very high quality of lessons'
>
> *Ofsted report, October 2005*

Most teachers recognise that students frequently know more about ICT than educational professionals, and the school has taken advantage of this by getting students to evaluate software for classroom use. Taking things several steps further, students are also now being encouraged to show teachers how to use more advanced features of the software, with widespread benefits. Later in the day, a group of students was also planning to feed back to Roger with comments on a free 3-D animation program they had been evaluating.

The school's innovative website is another example of a breakthrough achievement. It is replete with information, advice and other more advanced features that enable staff, parents and students to learn more about the school, keep up to date and access the curriculum within and outside school hours. A key part of the site for students is access to the Moodle VLE discussed earlier, allowing them to use a wealth of resources from home. A particularly interesting feature of the site is the posting of information and resources relating to specific courses, encouraging the students to interact with the website on a regular basis. The Snapshots Gallery is another important feature of the site, where photos of any school events can be uploaded. The professional nature of the website helps to show students that good design can be carried out in-house, and inspires them to get involved in making it even more impressive.

Significant investment has made the QES website professional, welcoming and a valuable learning resource in its own right

The hectic schedules of Roger and Mark, and their wider school responsibilities supporting colleagues, mean that a heavy teaching commitment would put undue pressure on them. An important decision, made possible partly through a series of new appointments in the ICT department, has been to allow them to use half their week to work on strategic ICT issues, rather than teach. This has accelerated other colleagues' use of ICT and helped the infrastructure and systems such as Moodle to provide a solid backbone for learning.

> *'Parents, pupils and members of the community rate the school very highly'*
>
> Ofsted report, October 2005

Confidence matters

The importance of *confidence* was singled out repeatedly during my visit. Roger and Mark are clearly authorities in their field and this has given them the ability to work towards their vision in the knowledge that they understand where they are going and—more importantly—exactly how they are going to get there. It has also helped them not to be intimidated by the fast pace of change in ICT education. An unswerving commitment to their mission has clearly helped to bring other staff behind their cause. But perhaps more critically than that, it has meant that when faced with external pressure to make unnecessary changes by the government or local agencies, the school has been able to resolutely defend what it is doing and why. It clearly helps that both Roger and Mark serve on high profile strategy groups in the region. These include Cumbria and Lancashire Education Online (CLEO), the regional Broadband Consortium, and the Cumbria ICT Strategy Group convened by the local authority. It is also apparent that other schools have benefited from their expertise and skills. Evidence of the leading edge work of the department includes the shortlisting of Mark in the 2004 BECTA

(British Educational Communications and Technology Agency) Best in Practice ICT Awards.

Over the last eight years the sharing of technical ICT knowledge has been an important aspect of the work of QES. The school now works in partnership with several others locally—for example, through the technical forum organised at local authority level. This is a very successful body which brings together technical staff from schools, the local authority and CLEO, and is a vital conduit in disseminating information and strategic developments. The paucity of appropriate ICT knowledge is often striking among schools, and the lack of appropriate expertise relating to real school issues even extends to so-called leading advisory bodies in the field. Roger and Mark are doing much to enhance ICT knowledge and understanding locally and regionally, and by looking outwards to help others, have gained considerable respect and influence.

It is clear that this confidence also comes through Roger and Mark's commitment to staying up to date with the latest developments in their field. The scale of the task should be not underestimated, given the fast pace of change in the ICT world. They are rigorous at maintaining their edge by attending briefings, browsing key websites, reading vital documents, contributing to online forums, attending relevant university courses and generally showing a very active interest in the changing landscape of ICT in schools. This, coupled with an almost obsessive attitude to progress, has enabled the creation of a unique ICT learning environment at QES. Not surprisingly, Roger and Mark are often asked to write articles about their work in CLEO, with Roger a major contributor to the CLEO *Across the Curriculum* professional file for schools.

I ended my visit to the ICT department with a whistle-stop tour of some of the latest hardware and software in use by students. This very practical demonstration, laid on by staff and students who spoke engagingly about their work, convinced me that Roger and Mark have done more than put ICT on the map at QES. They've breathed a real sense of *life* into the new technologies and helped to invigorate and enrich every subject area. Like alchemists working to produce rare metals from waste products, they've conjured up a kind of learning magic from hundreds of computer parts. A magic that was and is making a real difference to young lives in this beautiful corner of England.

> *'Students perceive their learning as fun and love coming to school'*
>
> Ofsted report, October 2005

Leadership matters too

Half a day of learning about the wholesale changes to the school made possible through ICT had left me rather weary. Roger and his team have taken ICT by the scruff of the neck and integrated it so successfully into learning that it seems like just another tool for teachers' use—albeit a tremendously powerful one. Example after example of highly effective work had been showcased before my eyes, and I was becoming intoxicated by the power of it all. I therefore welcomed the opportunity to spend some quiet time with headteacher Chris Clarke and his deputy Alison Hughes in order to learn more about the strategic aspects of ICT at QES. This was also an opportunity to ask some searching questions about how the school had achieved its success.

Chris has been in charge at QES for fifteen years, although the growth of the school during those years (from 650 to over 1,380 students) has made it feel like he has been leading three different schools over the period. Joining the school as a young and ambitious headteacher at the age of 38, he set to work immediately to help establish a firm sense of values that would underpin the school's efforts over the years to come. These are more than simply a guiding force for the work of the school: they form an essential set of core values to which staff—and students—can and do refer back to as necessary. This is illustrated by a recent assembly on the perennial school problem of chewing gum, or more accurately, the difficulty for cleaning staff in removing it from school premises. This was tackled not by lecturing students on what they should and shouldn't put in their mouths, or throw on the floor, but by showing images of the people responsible for removing the gum and referring back to the core school value of 'treating others decently'. This was introduced to the students in January as one of the school's 'New Year resolutions'.

The principal aim of my visit to the headteacher's office was to learn more about some of the leadership issues underpinning ICT use at the school. But one of the most intriguing and unexpected things to come out of my discussions with Chris and Alison was that the school enjoys a great deal of success across a multiplicity of areas. In September 2005 QES received an Ofsted report that every headteacher and governing body must pray for—the school was judged as 'outstanding' in every aspect. More recently, the school has received a number of accolades for its excellent examination results and has been invited to add a second (Modern Languages) and third (Training School) specialism to its performing arts status after much success in this area. This is clearly a very impressive school.

> *'The governing body, headteacher and leadership team set a vision for improvement which is realised through very effective management'*
>
> *Ofsted report, October 2005*

Queen Elizabeth School
Kirkby Lonsdale, Carnforth
Lancashire, LA6 2HJ

21 September 2005

Dear pupils and sixth form students

Thank you all so much for contributing to the recent inspection of your school, particularly to those amongst you who took the time to speak to us in interviews or just informally in the recreation areas. You will be delighted to know that the inspectors found that your school is outstanding. Your school is led by an excellent headteacher who is helped by the school governors, all teachers, pupils and students.

We found that you all make considerable progress in your learning and reach high standards. There are many reasons why you do so well at school. The teaching is excellent and your teachers plan exciting and challenging lessons. The inspectors also found that you were offered a great deal of choice of subjects and that many of you choose drama, art, dance, music and media studies.

We were very pleased to see that you were keen to participate in the numerous clubs and sports activities. I particularly enjoyed my visit to the Landscape Club and I do hope those bulbs grow! We noticed that many of you took the healthy eating option at lunchtime and this again told us a lot about your school and the way in which you have developed into mature individuals who are making wise choices.

The most important reason why you are doing so well is really down to you! You behave very well, and have excellent relationships with your teachers and with each other. You all look very smart and businesslike, and most importantly, come to school ready to work hard and do well.

Yours sincerely

Mary Sewell
Ofsted

My experience is that the road to educational excellence is not without its potholes, so I was eager to explore the leadership challenges that Chris had overcome in order to bring his school to its current position as one of Cumbria's most successful and respected schools. Not surprisingly, he confirmed that this success has not come overnight and is down mainly, in his view, to 'luck, good fortune, tenacity and a lot of hard work'. Chris identified a number of difficulties that the school has had to overcome in the last fifteen years. All of these required a cool head, a willingness to engage in positive discussion rather than hiding behind entrenched positions and a genuine belief that things *would* improve. One of the key challenges was to set up more robust systems and structures that would help the school to maintain its effectiveness in times of difficulty or change. The re-establishment of a clear set of shared values, especially the need for people to treat each other well and with respect as part of a community, engaged much of Chris's attention in his first few years in post. Slowly, and with much effort, things did begin to improve and the staff were able to set their sights on new objectives.

The school's reputation has always been good but the renewed efforts of Chris and his team, together with an appreciation that comprehensive status could attract a lot of new students from outlying areas of the catchment, led to an impressive growth in student numbers in the 1990s—a trend that has been maintained into the current decade. This has brought a range of benefits, including additional funding and buildings, a wider curriculum and the ability to attract new and talented staff with fresh ideas to a vibrant school. Personalisation of the curriculum has been made possible thanks to the high student numbers, which in year 12 and 13 results in a bewildering choice of study options, encompassing many non-traditional subjects such as Critical Thinking and World Development AS-levels.

A key challenge for the school in the future is how it maintains its success as it moves forward. The 'magic' that is detectable in the school is difficult to define and perhaps more difficult still to maintain. 'Being successful in many areas is a wonderful accolade, but it's also a burden,' Chris explains. If each successful aspect of the school is considered as a plate spinning on top of a pole, then it is not hard to imagine that a school such as QES has a tough job with so many plates spinning! The school needs to continually examine the elixir of forces that contribute to its success and try out new approaches, if it is not to allow some aspects of its practice to become stale.

> *'This excellent school has no major areas for improvement. It needs only to continue to maintain its high standards and to ensure that all pupils have every opportunity to maximise their potential'*
>
> Ofsted report, October 2005

Ethical approaches

Given the current successes of the school across the board you could be forgiven for thinking that this was an institution which actively sought to blow its own trumpet through national publicity and high profile links with business leaders, politicians and the great and good. But this is precisely what the school has chosen *not* to do—to its immense credit. Rather than spending time courting publicity and patting itself on the back for previous success, the school's focus remains firmly on its students. True to its motto, it is totally committed to ensuring present and future students benefit from the highest quality scholarship and care. The school's leaders are also aware of the need, when working in a federation, to sometimes allow other schools—which may be more hungry for positive publicity—to enjoy their place in the spotlight. This enlightened view of school promotion is just one example of the profoundly ethical approach that Chris injects into the school.

What also became clear is that Chris and his leadership team have done much to provide the conditions that have enabled the success of ICT and many other areas besides. Their aim, through the empowerment of others and respect for colleagues' expertise, has been to create 'rich soil' upon which excellence can grow. This has allowed staff to experiment without fear of failure, try unconventional approaches and do what, in their professional judgement, seems right without worrying about what Ofsted inspectors may think. Indeed, there's a tangible sense that the school cares much more about creating effective global citizens than it does about climbing the league tables—and the understated press comments on results day acknowledge that there are higher aims worth working towards than simply crude academic measures.

There is also a confidence that underpins the actions of leaders at the school that their staff *do* have the expertise and commitment to really make things happen. In return, colleagues certainly deliver—time and time again. Chris describes the staff as the most hard-working team he has ever worked with. Every day clubs, societies, action groups and after school enrichment activities augment an already rich curriculum. Crucially, teamwork is used very effectively in order to work towards maximum opportunity for all.

Clubs, societies and extra-curricular activities (May 2007)

Sport

Fencing
Kick Boxing
Yr 7 Rugby Union
Yr 8 Rugby Union
Yr 9 Rugby Union
Yr 10 Rugby Union
Yr 11 Rugby Union
1st XV Rugby Union
Yr 7 Football
Yr 8 Football
Yr 9 Football
Yr 10 Football
Yr 11 Football
Yr 7–9 Girls' Football
Yr 10–13 Girls' Football
Yr 8 & 9 Junior Netball
Year 7 Netball
Yr 10–13 Senior Netball
Yr 7 Hockey
Yr 8 & 9 Junior Hockey
Yr 9–13 Senior Hockey
Yr 10 & 11 Rugby League
6th Form Rugby League
6th Form Badminton
Yr 7–11 Badminton
Rock Climbing

Music/performing arts	Other
Yr 7 & 8 Drama Club	Game Design (IT)
String Orchestra	Duke of Edinburgh Bronze Level
Full Orchestra	
Clarinet Choir	Yr 7 School Council
Junior Flute Group	Christian Union
Senior Flute Group	Yr 7 Library Reading Club
Group Sight-singing	Yr 7 Crazy Club (Science)
Wind Orchestra	History Club
Lower Strings Ensemble	Food for Fun
Guitar Orchestra	Yr 8 & 9 Reading Club
String Quartet	People & Planet
Choir	Science for Gifted & Talented
Band Club	Amnesty International
Percussion Group	Yr 8 & 9 School Councils
Jazz Orchestra	Environment Action Group
Guitar Ensembles	Cipher Challenge Club (Maths)
Traditional Music Group	
Barbershop Group	
Brass Group	
Keyboard Group	
Saxophone Quartet	

My second discussion with Chris a few weeks later came just after he had been filmed for Teachers' TV, working with an A-level group on a literary criticism lesson. It is fitting, given the context for my visit to the school, that this lesson used as its stimulus an electronic discussion forum on the Jacobean tragedy *'Tis Pity She's a Whore* that the students had started reading during their Christmas holidays. Flushed with the frisson of excitement that comes from a successful lesson, Chris spoke excitedly about how ICT and Virtual Learning Environments in particular had re-energised his approach to teaching English literature. Through his personal engagement with ICT and its potential to transform teaching and learning, Chris was also sending out an important message to all staff—that for ICT to be truly embedded within the school its leaders needed to embrace it too. But more than that, Chris also demonstrated that school leaders can have a role in trialling and testing ICT as it gathers momentum in school.

Another key quality of the school's leaders—which is so clearly reflected in the attitudes of Roger Davies and his ICT team—is that they're prepared to admit they *don't* have all the answers. They're confident enough in what they *do* know to be clear where their expertise ends. This was manifested by a lesson of Roger's where students were being invited to give their views on the rising popularity of social networking sites such as Bebo, MySpace and Facebook, and the possible safety issues they raise. This potentially highly contentious issue was tackled not by teachers and school leaders saying they know best, but by a genuine dialogue with students on the way forward. This kind of approach has ensured that the school avoids knee-jerk reactions in favour of more considered approaches. By engaging with students, the hope is that lessons can be learnt by all. The lesson in question was also filmed by Roger and excerpts used during a later presentation he made to a local authority conference.

Letting the students speak

I ended my visit to QES by meeting with a group of students, mainly those on the Student Council that meets regularly to address concerns and plan initiatives. I was eager to find out what it is like to be a learner at the school.

The students confirmed much of what I had already heard from staff and what seems evident from the way the school community interacts. This is clearly an institution that students feel proud of and they certainly recognise many of its strengths. Indeed, when asked to suggest three things they would like to change about the school, some students could not think of any and many of those that could focused on the need for more social space for certain year groups outside lessons—something the school is hard pushed to do much about at present. The one area that had been troubling students—revised uniform regulations—appeared to fall into the category of a minor annoyance and a lack of understanding of the reasoning behind the new rules, rather than something that impinged on student well-being on a day to day basis. It's clear that the uniform concerns of students are not going to lead to a rebellion and I think it is telling that they are able to talk about the issue openly without fear of negative action being taken against them. Perhaps it's even healthy for students to have something they are united about, on which 'authority' is not able to compromise fully?

> ### Student opinions on QES
>
> 'It's a good school'
> 'It's welcoming'
> 'There's a buzz here'
> 'Any bullying is sorted out soon'
> 'There are lots of opportunities'
> 'There's always someone to talk to'
> 'The enthusiasm of teachers is great'

Queen Elizabeth School, Kirkby Lonsdale, is without doubt a school that has the 'wow factor'. Though my visit was primarily aimed at documenting the story of ICT, it could equally have been about pastoral care, respecting the student voice or a whole range of other topics. Excellence is the norm here. It's wonderful to spend time in a school that is so clearly achieving its goals, but where there's no hint of complacency over its success; to revel in leaders, teachers and students working together in a genuine partnership to achieve their goals, while also taking very seriously the shared ethics and values that underpin what they do.

The 'secrets' of success

Success at this outstanding school clearly did not happen by accident, and the following five factors seem to be the most significant ones underpinning its success.

Clear values uniting the school community

As headteacher, Chris Clarke has tried very hard to make QES an ethical, principled school. This is evident from his carefully considered editorials in the school magazine as much as it is from the manner in which he interacts with students. The school's values provide a constant source of strength and unity for the school community, and through consistency of message, have become part of the fabric that binds the school together.

Belief in people

I very much enjoyed the idea that leaders at QES strive to create 'rich soil' upon which staff can thrive. They clearly understand the need to have faith in people, to respect their expertise and to work together in a belief that they *will* be successful. The outstanding work of the ICT department could not have happened without Chris and other senior leaders being ready to admit that this was not their area of specialism, and allowing others to drive things forward.

Confidence—at many levels

QES is certainly a confident school, but this only comes about because staff have worked so hard to create such a solid foundation for their work. Roger spoke repeatedly about his work in ICT being underpinned by a real confidence in the new technologies. This has only been developed by a rigorous approach to Continuing Professional Development (CPD) and by going to great lengths to keep up with the latest developments in the subject. Confidence in ICT at QES also comes from Roger and Mark's membership of influential decision-making and strategic groups at authority and county level. There are many additional examples of this confidence from other aspects of the school, such as the award-winning quality drama productions, which have been possible only due to incredible attention to detail.

Careful planning

The ICT department has clearly benefited from the industrial background of its leaders. The strategic plans for ICT have a real flair, as well as a deep understanding of how the subject works in schools. They show exactly what needs to be done—and who needs to do it—for the school to move to the next level. Everyone is clear what part they must play, including the school's leaders. These plans are also guided by an exciting vision of ICT at QES, one that will see it at the leading edge of practice nationally.

Hard work and tenacity

These two factors were identified by Chris as major influences on the success of the school. They can easily be taken for granted, but more than that in some schools staff do not seem to fully understand what the words mean. It's clear that at QES Olympic levels of hard work and persistence are the norm, and this factor must not be underestimated when considering the school's success.

How transferable is this work?

One of the striking aspects of the work of QES is the *subject expertise* of Roger Davies and Mark McNulty. There's no doubt in my mind that much of the success of the school in ICT has been due to their intimate knowledge of hardware, software and appropriate teaching pedagogies. Their ability to work with high profile groups across the county and region has also cemented the position of ICT at the school. This underlines the fact that, in secondary schools at least, it is a real advantage to have in post teachers with strongly developed subject knowledge, as long as they can combine this with a deep understanding of teaching and learning. However, Roger warns against putting himself on a subject-expertise pedestal, recognising the personal learning journey he has taken. Commitment, in his view, has accounted for so much.

> 'My belief is anyone can do it. I have a politics degree and trained as a craft, design and technology teacher. Everything I have done has been self taught, through reading or attending extra courses—and if I can do it, so can anyone else; you just need a personal commitment to lifelong learning.' Roger Davies

There are many practical things that QES has done which could certainly be replicated in other schools. In particular, the identification of the four key challenges in ICT (technical, pupil, teaching, management) provides a template against which other schools can judge how far they have come, and where their priorities lay now. The strategic approach to actions once the challenges had been identified was a real hallmark of the department, and demonstrates how a highly focused approach can help to target limited resources. Again, this principle is easily transferable.

These 'secrets of success' contain many other messages of hope for schools more generally. Here, we have a set of principles that can be adapted to other contexts and circumstances, and would surely help to bring schools closer to success, whatever their current area of focus.

My visit to Cumbria had been more rewarding than I could have imagined. There was no doubt in my mind that the work taking place in Kirkby Lonsdale is very significant—as indeed are the achievements of its upland neighbour in Settle. The visit had only swelled my belief that there are many schools out there carrying out innovative practice whose stories need to be told. But I felt that if I was to produce a book charting comprehensively the success of schools —one that would persuade readers working in all kinds of settings— I needed to head next to a large city. Here I wanted to find a school that had emerged from challenging circumstances to achieve widespread acclaim in its urban community. The story of that school is told in the following chapter.

Chapter 3

Transforming a School in Challenging Circumstances

'Northumberland Park Community School is on a fantastic journey of success.' Andy Kilpatrick

I've often wondered what day to day life is like in a school in really challenging circumstances. I think such schools are places that can tell us a lot about what can and cannot be achieved in education. If leaders and teachers are able to transform schools in the most difficult of circumstances, then there is surely hope for every educational professional striving to make their schools better places in which to learn. I knew I had to include at least one example of such a school in this book. I was delighted to hear, therefore, about a school in north London that had undergone some dramatic developments in recent years. As soon as I could, I arranged an appointment to visit the school and headed down on a fast train to the capital.

I had only been in the staffroom for fifteen minutes and the sense of warmth among the staff of Northumberland Park Community School had already shone through. Groups of teachers talked enthusiastically through lesson plans, smiling and joking as they did so; others talked of having missed each other on days out; others still displayed the body language that shouts out that they really *care* about their colleagues. It was a lovely start to the day but it was to get even better when a charming year 11 student—Drew Evans—came in to the staffroom to collect me for my tour of the school. It had impressed me that he had found his way into the staffroom without the need to ask 'permission' from staff and I would soon see further examples of the relaxed and trusting relationship between staff and students at the school. The open door policy at the school means that students can frequently been seen chatting to the headteacher in his office about their progress and concerns.

Proud to be a student

As we explored the building, Drew pointed out the aspects of the school of which he was especially proud. He has his eyes set firmly on a career as a doctor, so we spent a lot of time in the science department, where he spoke passionately about the quality of the teaching and the creative ways in which teachers inspire young minds at Northumberland Park Community School. This includes bringing unconventional topics such as football right into the science classroom. The quality of the staff was mentioned time and time again. As we approached the English department he pointed out the classroom of the 'best English teacher in the country'. Further on during the tour we saw the music department at work, which is led by an incredibly dedicated teacher who is renowned for going that extra mile for students. Drew summarises his views on the teaching at his school in few simple words: 'We have the best of the best in teachers.'

The quality of *relationships* between staff and students was highlighted by Drew when he spoke of feeling that teachers are 'closer to friends than teachers'. This sentiment was also picked up by other students during the day, who suggested that some teachers seem to be acting almost as surrogate parents for students, always looking after their best interests. I have rarely heard young people speak more warmly of their teachers.

> *'This is a good school with a number of outstanding features'*
>
> Ofsted report, November 2006

At one point during the tour I had noticed an intriguing display showing the location of the home countries of teachers in one department. Later, the door to a classroom displayed the word 'welcome' in no less than ten languages. The multicultural heritage of the school, including of course its 1,024-strong student population, is clearly a key strength of Northumberland Park Community School. Drew spoke passionately about how well integrated students are at the school and the way in which young people are able to learn from each others' cultures. I was starting to get the feeling that this was an inclusive school—in the widest sense possible.

Notice on a classroom door

Welcome!

Kurdish	*Hun bi xer hatin*
Bulgarian	*Dobre doshli*
Bengali	*Shagatom*
Somali	*Soo dhawoow*
Spanish	*Bienvenidos*
Vietnamese	*Chào mung*
Tigrigna	*Enqai dehan mesakum*
French	*Bienvenue*
Arabic	*Merhaba*

'Most students are from minority ethnic groups. The main ethnic groups are of Turkish/Kurdish, White British and African or Caribbean heritage. Over sixty-two per cent do not speak English as their main language and a small minority are at an early stage of learning English. The group includes an increasing number with asylum or refugee status'

Ofsted report, November 2006

Drew pointed out through the window the nearby stands of White Hart Lane football ground, home to premiership team Tottenham Hotspur. The school's all-weather pitches are sometimes used by the club's Academy team during training.

I quizzed Drew a little more on the path to his chosen career in medicine and he was eager to point out that his academic studies had benefited greatly from a vocational course that he had followed thanks to the enlightened attitude of the school. His BTEC course in public services (clearly chosen to link to his future role as a doctor) sees him spending a day a week outside school at the nearby College of North East London studying subjects such as politics, citizenship and health. He recognises that this has built up his social skills as well as helping him to get out and meet new people. After taking his GCSEs in the summer, Drew plans to transfer to the nearby college to study for his A-levels.

As our tour came to an end I could not fail to be impressed by Drew's pride at being a student at Northumberland Park Community School. The tireless work of the staff have ensured that this highly motivated young man stands every chance of achieving his dream of becoming a doctor. The confidence of his statement that he 'will make it in medicine' is testament to the belief that staff clearly have in their students at this north London school.

High quality facilities at Northumberland Park Community School

Students at the school currently benefit from:

- An on-site swimming pool and sports complex, including outside AstroTurf, basketball and tennis courts
- A new art block and media suite
- New science laboratories
- Nine computer suites
- New technology and textiles workshops

- A well equipped library and study centre
- Music, drama, dance and assembly areas

A range of further developments are being planned that will provide students with some of the best learning facilities in the area.

Investing and believing in staff

Impressed by the warmth of relationships between staff, I was eager to find out more about the people dimension at Northumberland Park Community School. My guide through this aspect of the school's work was to be Linda Welds, assistant headteacher responsible for Continuing Professional Development, among other things.

As I chatted to Linda about staff development at the school, two key factors stood out: the school's willingness to invest in staff and also to genuinely believe in them. Northumberland Park Community School was one of the first in the country to engage with the graduate teacher programme and it now has a solid reputation as a centre of excellence for initial teacher training. The school is very much an example of how you really can 'grow your own talent', with a third of the current teaching staff having come through the school's own teacher training programmes, including the Advanced Skills Teacher in maths. This is clearly a superb school to be a newly qualified teacher.

One to one coaching has been an important part of work of Northumberland Park Community School in recent years. This has further helped to develop staff skills, as well as supporting the personal well-being of staff and allowing colleagues to discuss their development in a safe atmosphere. Lesson observation is also highly developed at the school, with the emphasis on the sharing of skills and the belief that we can all improve as teachers. A recent development has seen the school support the professional development of staff by offering access to a masters level qualification at no cost to the individual teachers.

Masters level study for Northumberland Park staff

The masters degree in education is run in conjunction with Middlesex University, with the school constituting an off-site centre. There are three elements to the course, each the focus of a year's part-time study:

Year 1: Developing professional practice
Year 2: Action enquiry for school improvement
Year 3: Dissertation

The university provides materials in the form of detailed guidance on how the research should be conducted, together with the assessment criteria. In addition to school-based sessions, participants get the chance to attend tutorials at the university on designated Saturdays during the year. There is also the opportunity for detailed online feedback on their work.

Students direct what is studied at each phase of the course, based on their interests. The focus for the research may stem from a personal, departmental or school-based issue. Some of the recent research topics have included deep questioning, developing teaching for more able students, coaching and the use of ICT. Each person taking the course is part of a mutually supportive group, with everyone's work discussed and ideas and guidance offered.

Through the masters course the school has achieved some excellent results in terms of the research carried out and in terms of career development and school improvement.

The success of the school in this area means that it is recognised in London for the high quality of teaching and learning it provides. While it has always had good staff, the leadership team recognise the need for continual improvement and constantly invest in developing new skills, embedding them and then moving on to the next area.

One example is the school's recent work to improve assessment for learning across the curriculum. The benefits of this work were noted in the school's most recent Ofsted inspection, which found that professional development has been a key factor in developing the capacity of middle managers as well as teachers.

> 'Our fantastic journey of success demands that we have well-ordered classrooms, with well planned and expertly delivered lessons. All teaching is closely monitored and meets our rigorous standards.' Northumberland Park Community School prospectus

The work of the school to develop a strong and highly skilled workforce has led to other benefits. There is a very low turnover rate among staff at a time when other schools in the capital are finding it hard to recruit and retain teachers. Teachers clearly settle in easily in a school where they are made to feel welcome and valued. The role of support staff is also valued and demonstrated through their active involvement in a range of developments. One example is the work of the head's personal assistant, Elaine Neacy, in one to one counselling work with students, harnessing her skills as a qualified professional counsellor.

Linda spoke repeatedly about the dedication of staff, helping to confirm Drew's earlier remarks on the willingness of colleagues to go that extra mile for students. A rich array of clubs and other extra-curricular activities are organised to enrich the curriculum—indeed, this provision was judged as 'outstanding' in the most recent Ofsted inspection. Significantly, staff are also increasingly taking educational risks in order to improve learning, while striving to see the child—not the behaviour—if things go wrong.

The depth of the work carried out at the people level has meant that Northumberland Park Community School is a rare example of a school with genuine emotional intelligence. And the students are reaping the rewards of this on a day to day basis.

Leading the learning journey

Andy Kilpatrick is certainly one of the most down-to-earth headteachers I have ever met. As we shall see later this is one of the keys to his success, but I wanted to find out more about the journey that Northumberland Park Community School had undergone in the last five years. As we settle down in his office over tea and biscuits I soon begin to get a sense of how much determination has been needed to overcome the many challenges the school has faced. It is a sad fact that a few years ago more young men went to prison than to university in this part of north London, which is one of the most deprived wards in Greater London.

'In 2003 the school was in serious trouble,' explains Andy who is currently in his third headship. 'The school had been issued with a Section 15 notice and was identified by the local authority as having no capacity for improvement. This followed a five year period during which the number of students gaining five or more higher grade passes remained static at nineteen per cent. There was a clear risk of the school being closed and reopened as an Academy. At that time an acting head was doing his best to tackle the school's problems, following the departure of the previous head, but the future of the institution was uncertain.'

By 2004 some improvements had been made, with the percentage of students getting five GCSE passes at grades at C or above rising to twenty-seven per cent, but progress was painfully slow. Andy joined the school in September 2004 and was quite clear that his key task was the further improvement in results, helping to open up opportunities to young people who had been denied them because of poor results in the past. The depth of the challenges facing the school at this time meant that this would require a series of quite radical measures—something that Andy was not afraid to tackle head on.

First to be targeted was student behaviour. A clear message needed to be sent out that it was not acceptable for other students' learning to be affected by poor behaviour. This resulted in a very high level of fixed term exclusions for a short period of time, which often tested the resilience of staff, students and parents. Thankfully though, rapid improvements in behaviour resulted, allowing staff to concentrate more and more on improving teaching and learning.

A better curriculum at Key Stage 4 was seen as another vital step. The goal was to improve students' motivation for learning and this was achieved partly by adopting a series of new vocational courses that appealed to students' interests and aptitudes. These ran alongside conventional courses, providing a distinctive mix of courses to help personalise the learning journeys of students.

> *'Its standing in the local community has increased because now behaviour is good and there is a strong emphasis on raising standards. The school's rapid recovery after a very difficult period led, for the first time, to a demand for places at the start of the new academic year'*
>
> Ofsted report, November 2006

Courses to enrich the curriculum

In addition to GCSEs, students in year 10 and 11 get the opportunity to study nationally recognised vocational qualifications, some in partnership with post-16 education providers. These courses include:

- Engineering
- Construction
- Hairdressing
- Music technology
- Media
- Design
- Science
- Art
- PE

The third area of focus was the exhaustive monitoring of student progress, coupled with rigorous target setting and a willingness to implement bold interventions to bring students back on track. This aspect of the school's work is led by Dave Spring, the assistant head responsible for data analysis and tracking, who the headteacher describes as the 'best data person in the capital'.

Andy believes there are three types of school when it comes to data. First there are *data poor* schools where there is simply not enough data available to make informed decisions about what to do differently. Second there are *data rich* schools, where much information may be available but the story ends there. Finally there are *data responsive* schools—those that really use data in order to improve outcomes for young people. He believes that schools can only be successful if they fall into the final category. However, to use data effectively there also needs to be a great system in place to make it work for the school and a highly skilled leader to provide overall coordination. The school has clearly found such a leader in Dave Spring who manages a highly effective information management system which provides a platform for the recording and use of data, underpinned by user-friendly software and hardware. This allows a range of analyses to be conducted that help to show what interventions should be made by the school (see below).

Student data at Northumberland Park Community School

Example: year 11 analysis

Each year Dave Spring uses the school's information management system to find out which year 11 students are not on target to obtain five GCSE passes at grade A*–C. Using data from trial exams and the latest teacher assessments, a list is drawn up of students who appear to be on the borderline between a C and D grade. For each of these students a carefully planned personalised strategy is devised. This may encompass extra support, changing sets or teaching groups, one to one discussions or mentoring and coaching work. The simple fact that these youngsters get 'targeted student status' seems to make some difference to their performance in itself. The school provides three progress reports to parents each year, each complemented by a progress meeting. The school then looks at their final grades to evaluate how effective the interventions were, providing valuable data for the following year's analysis.

Dave explains that one of the major successes in using data has been to do real things with data and make it part of the day to day life of teachers. The inputting of data on examinations and teacher assessments, for example, generates predicted grades that help to make teachers more accountable. In turn they become better at accurately predicting students' achievements, which is key to planning appropriate interventions. It is far from being just a paper exercise. Naturally, high quality target setting is also made possible through the school's rigorous approach to data. Two kinds of targets are set for students: a base line target and a more challenging one. This provides a very useful tool for assessment of learning activities, which help students to work towards the more challenging target. Timetabling is also seen as a key tool to help address underachievement of individuals. A radical model is employed whereby the school is re-timetabled up to six times a year to ensure the best possible mix of subjects and teachers. The advanced use of student data at Northumberland Park Community School is starting to turn heads across London. The school has made presentations to several other schools and is clearly regarded as a beacon of good practice in this area.

> *'The good curriculum with its excellent vocational and work-related courses ensures that students gain validated and valuable qualifications. The courses are carefully matched to students' needs and interests. The vocational courses including the personalised work-related programme for some students are outstanding features of the curriculum'*
>
> Ofsted report, November 2006

The school's work using student data is complemented by a determined effort to build partnerships with parents. This includes regular reports, progress meetings and a genuine open door policy for parents. Andy Kilpatrick has taken the unusual step of making himself available to talk to parents between 6 and 7 p.m. on two evenings a week, helping to form strong bonds for the benefit of students. High quality newsletters and a recently overhauled—and regularly updated—website also help parents keep up to date with school life. The school aims to place parents 'in the driving seat' by fully involving them in the life of the school. Family learning activities go one step further by helping parents develop their skills and gain qualifications, thus allowing them to support their children's learning more effectively.

Andy recognises that headteachers often feel pulled in all sorts of directions by government initiatives, local authority projects and other external forces. He quickly learned that you have so say 'no' to the right things—those that will take you further from your goals rather than closer to them. This can be challenging and requires that you constantly have to justify what you are doing and why you are doing it. One example comes in the form of a recent visit from an external organisation to determine the school's special provision for Somali students. It came as something of a surprise to the visitors when Andy announced that there were no projects under way that were specifically targeted at this single student group. A greater surprise lay in store when Andy explained that the achievement of Somali students at Northumberland Park Community School was the highest that had ever been recorded from a UK school! How could this apparent anomaly have occurred? Quite simply because the school's data monitoring had picked up the potential underachievement of students (including those Somali students at risk of not meeting their targets) early on and it had implemented successful interventions that brought these students back on track. Northumberland Park Community School is now considered a model school for its use of student data and has been used as a case study of a school that is highly successful at working with students from minority ethnic groups.

> 'We are very proud of our school and showing it off to parents/carers and prospective students is a great pleasure.' Northumberland Park Community School prospectus

This is just one example of the way in which Northumberland Park Community School is ahead of the crowd in so many ways. Its expertise in the use of student data means that it does not have to drop everything to join in with the latest government scheme. It is already many steps ahead.

The effects of all the above work on the examination results at Northumberland Park Community School have been spectacular. By 2007 the percentage of students getting five GCSE grades of A*–C was up from nineteen per cent in 2003 to seventy per cent, with key gains in English and maths. This has led to no less than five letters of congratulation from government ministers and has seen the school placed as the seventh most improved school nationally in 2006. The data for 2007 look set to place the school in the top ten nationally for its Contextual Value Added score, an indication of the additional benefit that students gain from attending Northumberland Park Community School.

I am keen to explore in more detail the factors that have brought about these profound changes and Andy is very conscious of the vital role of what he calls 'change agents' in his school. These are the staff who are taking a very active role in rapidly accelerating the school towards a brighter future. Such staff seem to possess an insight into what children really need—either in the classroom or beyond. More and more staff at Northumberland Park Community School are now taking on the mantle of being change agents, and this is clearly making a huge difference to the overall success of the school.

Andy's own experiences of education have also provided him with some unique insights into what it is like to be a student who is not fully engaged by school. 'Most teachers don't understand failure,' he explains. 'As a youngster growing up in rural Wiltshire having failed my 11-plus, I have a good understanding of what it means to be disconnected from learning and this gives me an edge. It enables me to see things from the students' point of view.'

I wanted to explore how the school measured its success at a time when examination results have hit all time highs at Northumberland Park Community School. Andy was very clear that academic success was important but that the school was also passionate about developing the skills of students as human beings. Paramount here was their ability to grow up expecting society to be a diverse place, populated by people with varied backgrounds and abilities. Andy is mindful of the debate over whether examination results are the true measure of success for a school, but feels you cannot get away from the fact that examination grades do make a difference when it comes to access to higher level courses or the world of work. He feels there is much basic work to do before the playing field for the young people in this part of London can be levelled.

Throughout our discussions, Andy is at pains to point out that he really *loves* his job. This might seem like an obvious criterion for any head, but like Andy I have worked with quite a few heads who do not seem to enjoy the day to day challenges of the role. Some of these people prefer to stay within the confines of their own or other people's offices 'being busy'. Instead, Andy makes a big effort to get out and about in his school and talk to staff and students, and does his best to instil belief in everyone that this is a school that is going to succeed—that success here is the norm. This hands-on style of leadership is clearly the hallmark of this charismatic headteacher.

> 'By making academic achievement and students' progress the driving force behind our extraordinary journey of success, we have become one of the most improved schools in the country.'
> Northumberland Park Community School prospectus

An inclusive school

Throughout my visit to the school the degree to which the needs of individuals are respected kept manifesting itself. From one to one mentoring through to whole class teaching, this is clearly a school that really understands and models inclusion. Its vision to be a fully inclusive school is no doubt helped considerably by the presence on site of The Vale, a vibrant 'school within a school' providing education to children with special educational needs, all contained entirely within the walls of Northumberland Park Community School. To any visitor and to students alike, it is like the two schools are joined as one. In my discussions with students The Vale was mentioned repeatedly as an important feature of the school. One year 11 girl said that having The Vale on site opened her eyes to respecting young people with disabilities more and helped her to appreciate their needs. Another student, a boy, said that even the 'bad boys' step aside to let those in wheelchairs make their way through the corridors.

> 'One of the school's outstanding strengths lies in the high level of respect and understanding students show when working in lessons and moving around the site with students from The Vale School. The collaborative work with the school is exemplary'
>
> Ofsted report, November 2006

Vale School—'the best of both worlds'

The Vale is a pioneering and innovative special school catering for children aged 2–19 with physical disabilities and associated special educational needs. There are eighty students on roll who come from Haringey and four neighbouring boroughs.

The Vale opened in 1924 on premises that had become unsuitable by the end of the twentieth century, so in 1997 the school relocated to new purpose built accommodation located on the same site as Lancasterian Primary School and Northumberland Park Community School. The accommodation and facilities at these two sites is of the highest quality and includes therapy areas and a hydrotherapy pool.

Taking advantage of the site, students at The Vale are included in the life and curriculum of the partner schools, and all sites are fully wheelchair accessible. The school provides an individually tailored curriculum within a context of inclusive education.

Another distinctive feature of The Vale are the inclusion schemes run in conjunction with Northumberland Park Community School. These were developed in the late 1970s and early 1980s, pioneering the inclusion of students with physical disabilities into mainstream schools, and have attracted national recognition and attention. Vale teaching and support staff ensure access by providing a blend of physical, emotional and learning support. They also liaise and work in partnership with Northumberland Park colleagues to ensure that the students have the optimum conditions to access and benefit from the mainstream courses. Tutor groups within The Vale are also linked with their mainstream peers for collaborative projects and activities.

The Vale extends its role by providing an advice and consultation service to all mainstream schools within Haringey.

'In exchange for their crumbling building, the students have become part of lively school communities, all of which have been painstakingly designed to meet their many requirements.' Times Educational Supplement

We Did It Here!

Chapter 3: Transforming a School in Challenging Circumstances | 95

Student success in all its forms is celebrated at Northumberland Park Community School

It is clear that inclusion is an important theme underpinning much of the work of this diverse school. Across the school support systems are in place for every culture and need and staff really care about individuals. This extends to the headteacher, whose students know that he *has* got time for them.

> '*Providing each and every student with challenging and creative learning opportunities within an environment of support and in partnership with parents.*' Northumberland Park Community School prospectus

The student voice

I needed to find out more about day to day life as a student at Northumberland Park Community School, so I decided to have lunch with five year 11 students who were happy to speak about their school. It quickly became clear that they had a lot of pride in their school, mirroring the sentiments of their fellow year 11 student Drew who had first shown me round the school.

I had noticed how quiet and calm the classrooms seemed to be as students worked and I was intrigued to know more about this. I was told, by several of those present, that teaching is a huge strength of the school and the classrooms only tend to get noisy when the students are excited about their learning! Several examples of fun approaches to learning were then readily mentioned by the students, across many curriculum areas.

The students explained about the role of the student council and their views on which aspects of the school could be improved—for example, the need for a greater range of food in the canteen, more specialised equipment in classrooms and student lockers. Crucially, there were no criticisms of people or systems at the school. Indeed, one girl explained how she had recently stuck up for her school when criticisms were made by students from another part of London—and the other students in the group then quickly sprang to her defence, making it clear that they too felt strongly about the success of Northumberland Park Community School. Such comments make it clear that these students clearly care about their school and are not afraid to say so.

> 'Students see their school as a happy place and speak compellingly about the benefits they have gained from the changes. Although the social circumstances of many students are complex, the school is a vibrant place in which students' personal development and well-being are good'
>
> Ofsted report, November 2006

The students were also united in their praise of headteacher Andy Kilpatrick, believing him to be a most approachable headteacher who really cared about their future. Several spoke warmly about their lunchtime conversations with Andy as he tours the school, keeping in touch with day to day issues and making personal contact with students. Finally, the community nature of the school was singled out by the students as an important feature of their school. The school's facilities, notably its swimming pool and all-weather pitches, are frequently used by neighbouring schools, especially primaries that are not so well equipped.

The 'secrets' of success

We turn now to consider more systematically the factors that have enabled Northumberland Park Community School to achieve its current success. While we need to be mindful here that there is no universal mechanistic blueprint for success in struggling schools, I do believe that there are some general principles that have enabled the school to achieve success, and which are very relevant to other schools. Six factors in particular seem to stand out.

A smart focus on data

It is clear that the use of data on student performance at this London school is cutting edge. The ability of the school to spot patterns of underachievement, and then back them up with tangible interventions that really make a difference, mark this school out. But more than that, the rigorous approach to data analysis at the school is also helping it to be cutting edge in terms of its inclusion work. Monitoring of students, at the *individual* level, means that every student is being enabled to reach their potential in a very focused way. The impressive results of students in groups that traditionally have underachieved in British schools—for example, Somali students and those from African-Caribbean heritage—are testament to the effectiveness of the use of student data at Northumberland Park Community School.

Being true to a core mission

Staff at Northumberland Park Community School are very clear about the school's core mission to improve life opportunities for young people in Haringey. They are also clear about the strategies that will be used to ensure this mission is accomplished. The leadership of the headteacher has been especially significant in this area, as he has resisted the efforts of outside agencies to follow agendas which are deemed necessary by those external to the school. Instead, he has enabled the school to cut through what is often a very complex web of government strategies and local authority priorities to find a very clear path to school improvement—one focused on the needs of individual students. Andy is adamant that if you have a good team of staff working with students in the right environment, then success will follow. His ability to simplify the mission of the school in a practical, down-to-earth way has clearly been very significant in uniting people behind a tangible cause.

'The school's success in helping students to make excellent progress is linked to the headteacher's outstanding leadership and management skills. The headteacher knows the client groups and has been exceptionally effective in ensuring that staff understand his vision for the school's future development'

Ofsted report, November 2006

Being bold with innovations

The ladder to success at Northumberland Park Community School has been punctuated with a series of often radical measures that have been taken to fast track the school to a brighter future. Some, such as the very strict policy on exclusions during the first few years of Andy Kilpatrick's headship, caused some turmoil for staff and the school community, but they were necessary to bring order to classrooms. The school's willingness to change the curriculum for students who are underachieving, often in quite radical ways, is another example of how bold innovations have brought profound rewards. While some staff found the transition difficult, none now question the actions that are being taken to improve the educational prospects for young people at Northumberland Park Community School. Indeed, success is now the norm at the school, and this brings with it an expectation that bold steps will continue to be necessary to tackle the challenges of the future.

Investing in staff

There are some striking examples of how Northumberland Park Community School has invested in people capital—most notably in training teachers to become even more effective in the classroom. Posts for Advanced Skills Teachers, teaching and learning coordinators, and teaching and learning mentors are all clear signals that teaching and learning really matter at this school. This is backed up with a range of professional development—from the coaching of individuals to a group of teachers engaging in a masters level course—all designed to equip teachers with the skills to make an even greater difference in the classroom. The comments of students on the quality of teaching at the school, together with the now outstanding examination results, provide solid evidence that this investment in staff is paying dividends. The school has also benefited from a leading practitioner in the training of teachers in the form of assistant headteacher Linda Welds. She has also helped to nurture a distinctive emotional intelligence among staff, that is noticeable even on a brief visit to the school.

Trusting staff and students

The headteacher has made a concerted effort to distribute leadership among key staff and then stand back and allow them to take responsibility. Andy is very much in favour of 'outcome management' rather than people management, allowing individuals to work towards improvements in the knowledge that they won't be subject to constant interference. This requires trust in staff and an ability to let go of many initiatives that were originally the head's idea. Examples include the use of student data, which is now expertly led by Dave Spring who developed into the role having become interested in this aspect of schools' performance after attending a course. Students too are trusted in a range of ways, resulting in a relaxed atmosphere between staff and students that can be rare in urban settings.

Thinking positively

One of the key attributes of Andy Kilpatrick is a clear belief that things will be successful and that determination will bring success. This drives Andy to be very decisive and to 'get on and do it' after making an assessment of the risks. The conflicting demands on the 'head time' of our school leaders means that they are sometimes drawn into negative thinking, especially when confronted by a range of new government initiatives. This is clearly not a feature of Northumberland Park Community School. One member of staff spoke of the school achieving 'substantial gains through a huge effort', summing up nicely a key principle that binds staff together and helps them to be optimistic when confronted with new challenges.

How transferable is this work?

Seeing a successful school at work can be an exhilarating experience, especially when that school has emerged from very challenging circumstances to enjoy widespread acclaim in its community. As I reflected on the progress that Northumberland Park Community School has made since 2003 I wanted to know more from the key people behind this transition on the extent to which, in their view, the work of the school was transferable to other institutions. I quizzed staff time and time again on this matter and received the same reply every time: the principles that the school has used to achieve success can—categorically—be used by other schools to create a brighter future for young people.

As he spoke about the work of the school over the last four years, Andy talked repeatedly about the quality of his staff, shying away from his own role in the school's transformation. However, I am convinced that progress would have been much slower had this school not been blessed with such a skilled and visionary leader—indeed, the school may have been forced to close in the mid-1990s. Conversations with other staff during the day confirmed the fact that Northumberland Park Community School is a living example of the notion that 'exceptional schools need exceptional leaders'.

Having been inspired by a school in the capital that has emerged from challenging circumstances, I wanted to find out more about the specifics of teaching and learning in a contrasting part of the country. I was especially interested to explore the extent to which a distinctive school culture focused on learning can play a central role in creating a successful school. An innovative school I was aware of in Rochdale seemed to fit the bill perfectly, so I headed over the Pennines to find out more.

'Parents rightly feel that since the headteacher's appointment, the school has been transformed'

Ofsted report, November 2006

Andy Kilpatrick—very much a hands-on headteacher

Chapter 4

Let's Focus on Learning

> 'Learning is power.' Andy Raymer, headteacher, Matthew Moss High School, Rochdale

Excellence in school leadership can have many manifestations. It can be displayed through a visionary approach to running an institution; by a complete mastery of the people skills needed to achieve a collective dream; or through an ability to build a high quality team that gets results. But it can also come from the ability to simplify the complex, to focus on a core aim—a single aim—that has such utter clarity and seems so logical that one cannot believe that all schools are not queuing up to ascribe to that same goal. Andy Raymer, headteacher of Matthew Moss High School in Rochdale, displays this rare ability more than any school leader I've met. Though he describes himself as 'a bit of a maverick' and as 'unemployable elsewhere' he has worked tirelessly to create a living, breathing example of what a school should look like which places learning at the heart of everything it does. The results are written vividly on the faces of the students from this 900-strong 11–16 school, which serves a socially and ethnically diverse part of Rochdale—one of Lancashire's many former mill towns. So much so, that some of these same students have gone on record to say that they hope Mr Raymer is now unemployable elsewhere, because they do not want to lose him as their headteacher!

I had got to know the work of Matthew Moss High School during a research project I was engaged in, which began in the autumn of 2006. Though the focus for my work had been to analyse some innovative teaching methods being used in the history department, it quickly became clear that this was no ordinary school. Specially prepared posters adorned the walls of every classroom, charting the learning behaviours and attributes that students would need to display in order to be successful. Young people arrived ready to learn and engaged in highly stimulating lessons with an enthusiasm that is rare to find in contemporary classrooms. But the most tangible demonstration of the unique character of the school came through the *language* that could be heard in every classroom—a language focused on learning. Both teachers and students spoke repeatedly in terms of *what* they were learning, *how* they were learning it and *why* they were learning those things. Incidences of poor behaviour were spoken of not in terms of sanctions and reprisals, but were measured by the impact that misdemeanours were having on the learning of others.

> '*Teachers have a very good understanding of how students learn, so they match the teaching method to students' needs very well*'
>
> Ofsted report, June 2005

Many schools claim that they are ultimately places of learning, but none has surely embraced this notion more passionately than Matthew Moss High School. Everywhere you go in this school, whoever you speak to, the evidence is there to be seen and heard. And it doesn't just stand out—it leaps out from every nook and cranny, and grabs you by the scruff of the neck. It proclaims loudly that this is a school where creative teaching and learning approaches unite all staff and students—put quite simply in the words of headteacher Andy Raymer, because 'learning is power'.

As soon as I was able to free up some time from my work in the history department, I went in search of the story of this unique school, finding key people to talk to and examples to illuminate what they had to say. Slowly, the path the school has followed began to reveal itself.

A new start

Matthew Moss High School opened in 1990 as a new-build institution on the site of a former middle school, part of a major reorganisation of the primary-middle-high school system across Lancashire. Andy Raymer joined the school as headteacher a few months before he opened the doors to its first intake of students, and was joined by a number of the most influential staff who still walk its corridors to this day. Immediately, work began to embed a distinctive culture of learning into the school. Right from the beginning Andy had faith that the young people at the school would learn successfully with the appropriate *stimulus*. This was based on Andy's first-hand experience of innovative approaches to learning. He had been particularly inspired by some highly creative teaching in humanities at his previous school led by an influential mentor (Mike Davies). This work involved students playing a very active role in learning through an integrated humanities curriculum, rather than learning passively behind desks in classrooms. A key feature of this work was to develop a curriculum that dealt with important concepts, rather than having a curriculum for its own sake. Further inspiration came in the form of drama specialist Tim O'Grady, who demonstrated the power of drama in explaining difficult concepts. These early influences convinced Andy that if students are fully *engaged* in lessons, they will learn. So, on joining Matthew Moss High School, Andy saw genuine student engagement in a curriculum of real substance as key to the success of the school.

Andy is convinced that learning is a multi-dimensional and multi-faceted experience. While accepting his responsibility to foster high quality learning in his school, he was also aware that learning takes place *outside* the school gates too. In the early days of the school there was a tangible feeling that there would not be another opportunity like this to agree the ethos and direction of the school. And staff readily seized the opportunity to clarify the key principles that would underpin the work of Matthew Moss High School in the years ahead. An important principle to emerge during these early days was the notion that learning will take place more readily if there's an absence of fear—and that young people need to be taught how to think in order not to fear failure. Students at the school were going to be encouraged to say 'Of course I can', rather than 'I can't'.

> *'The school is very successful in developing positive attitudes to learning and achievement in its students'*
>
> Ofsted report, June 2005

Andy's principal leadership role model is US business leader W. Edwards Deming, whose fourteen principles for effective organisations have given the school the 'intellectual permission' to try out many techniques that appealed to Andy's innate sense of what seemed right for his school.

The five key aims of Matthew Moss High School

1. To develop and sustain an atmosphere in which learning is successful and is enjoyed.
2. To establish, for all students, entitlement and access to a broad and balanced curriculum, based on a commitment to equality of opportunity.
3. To sustain a caring, supportive atmosphere within a framework of personal growth, developing each person's sense of worth, responsibility and self-discipline.
4. To enable the school to operate effectively at the heart of the community.
5. To sustain an atmosphere in which students take pride in their work, their school and their community, within an ethos of high expectations that sees us all striving for success.

Progress through innovation

Andy is certainly prepared to buck the trend of the increasing number of schools that seem obsessed with targets and rigorous structures. Indeed, his maverick reputation—in truth, I think, fuelled by an admiration that this is a single-minded leader who is not prepared to give lip service to the latest, usually ephemeral, government initiatives—is based partly on his belief that 'systems interfere with progress'. Instead, the whole community is clear that this is a school whose main passion is for learning in its widest sense: everything else is seen as peripheral. On his first morning at the school, Andy can distinctly remember hearing one teacher say 'We've got a trendy', as the new head outlined his distinctive vision for the school. Judging by the success of Matthew Moss High School fifteen years on, more school leaders ought to emulate Andy's trendy leadership style.

His goal, obviously something new to many staff, was to give teachers permission to experiment, innovate and take risks, without fear of blame or retribution. Moreover, the school continues to work tirelessly to create a 'no blame' culture. Teachers, for example, are not taken to task for 'failure' to meet targets; instead a professional dialogue takes place about how learning can be improved. Creativity is a theme that genuinely unites staff and Andy firmly believes that everyone enjoys expressing their creative skills and gains personal satisfaction from doing so.

The fact that innovation is so clearly valued by the school's leadership team is evident in the school development plan. Far from the usual dull tables replete with educational jargon, Matthew Moss High School's plan is brought to life as a colourful and inspiring mind map.

108 | We Did It Here!

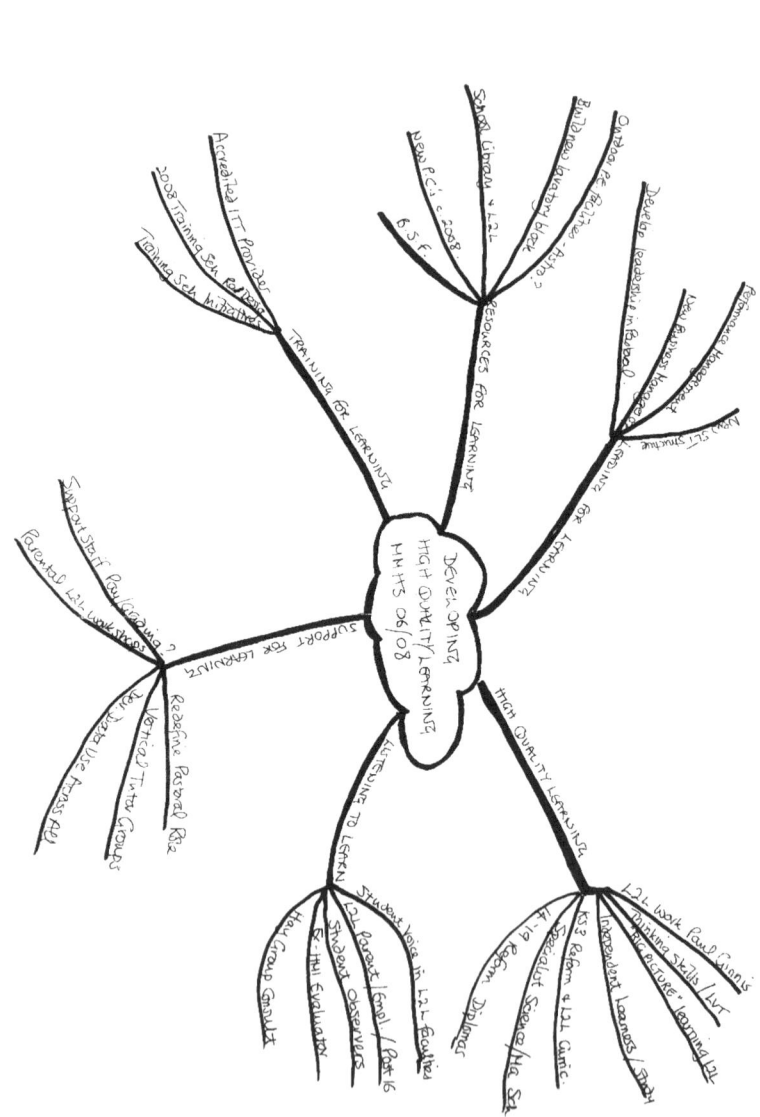

Development planning—Matthew Moss style

Another factor singled out as significant by Andy is the *constancy of purpose*. There has been tireless work at a variety of levels to reinforce positive messages about learning at every opportunity. There is also a feeling that this is a school that *celebrates* learning and success in the classroom for its own sake, rather than by being measured simply by crude indices.

Elsewhere in the school, additional inspiration oozes from other key staff. A key partner in achieving positive change has been Andy's deputy head Geraldine Norman. Geraldine's contribution to the school's success is clearly very significant. Her commitment to innovation in learning can be illustrated by the unusual topic of her research project for the Established Leaders course run by the National College for School Leadership—the use of students as critical observers of lessons. Though many of her colleagues on the course, from other schools, cast doubt on the idea that students could be trained as observers—and fewer still believed that these young people could provide insightful comments that would help teachers to improve their practice—the success of her work can be seen today in the team of highly skilled student observers now 'in post' at the school, some of whom I interviewed later in day.

The school's focus on learning enables it to be robust to many of the external pressures impacting on education institutions today. So, instead of having designated meetings to discuss, for example, the Key Stage 3 Strategy, the school has discussion groups to explore how the strategy might enhance learning. A simple motto that binds staff together is 'Let's devote our time to the things that matter'. And by doing so, the school is empowering its students every day to become effective global citizens. There is a sense that there's a bigger mission at work here—to help students to develop the skills, knowledge and habits of mind that will ensure that they are first and foremost *lifelong learners*, who, in the words of Geraldine Norman, 'will be able to cope easily with a few GCSEs thrown at them in year 11'.

The school's leaders recognised early on that if staff and students were to be united by a passion for learning, then they needed a common language for learning, a *language* that everybody understood and was comfortable using. A working group of staff set to work to create that language, the fruits of which surprise every visitor to the school in the way they startled me on my first visit. Teachers clearly strive to make language about learning a significant feature of every lesson at the school.

Through effective teamwork Matthew Moss High School has successfully established a distinctive learning culture in the school, which has allowed it to enjoy considerable success locally and further afield. The progress of the school led to two important milestones at a critical stage in its development—being awarded Beacon School and Training School status in 2000, and subsequently being invited to join the Leading Edge Schools programme in 2003. These milestones provided valuable external validation that the school was indeed achieving impressive results through its innovative approaches.

> *'The school is a Leading Edge school, which means it has been chosen as part of a national initiative to help other schools improve the quality of education they provide. The school plays a leading role in training new teachers through its recognition as a Designated Recommending Body'*
>
> *Ofsted report, June 2005*

Learning from others

Several influential figures have played a role in the shaping of the educational ethos and methods of the school since the early years. They include Anthony Gregorc, an early pioneer of learning styles analysis, who worked decades before the term 'accelerated learning' was invented. Eager to inspire staff and connect directly with leading thinkers and best-selling authors in education, the school did not shy away from inviting internationally known figures to work face to face with staff. These included Spencer Kagan, Kathleen Butler, Dean

Fink and Paul Ginnis (author of *The Teacher's Toolkit*, and from whom we shall hear later). Each consultant gave something different to the school and some are continuing their relationship with Matthew Moss High School in order to help staff create an even more powerful learning community. Through this exposure to leading authorities in their fields, the school became a pioneering exponent of the Learning to Learn agenda, way ahead of its time.

> *'The school has focused its attention very strongly on learning and this focus has been intensified through the Learning to Learn programme. In lessons there are fast-paced activities that change frequently. Many different activities are used, to ensure that there is something in the lesson for all students that is optimised to the way that they learn best'*
>
> Ofsted report, June 2005

The school also wished to learn from successful schools elsewhere and numerous visits were arranged to see good practice in action. Significantly, this included witnessing the work of Cramlington Community High School in Northumberland, which has received much attention through the school's high profile books, including *Creating an Accelerated Learning School*, a work co-authored by the headteacher and head of science. Though it was eager to learn from outstanding practice elsewhere, the school was no stranger to innovative teaching methods that had been developed *inside* the institution. It adopted the Somerset Thinking Skills course years before such approaches received widespread recognition through high profile government reports and the Key Stage 3 Strategy. Educational links further afield have also enriched the school. Most recently, collaborative work with a South African school has bridged cultural and geographical barriers in order to bring fresh approaches to a range of teaching and learning challenges.

From its foundation the school has felt a need to nurture the next generation of school teachers through its extensive training work. Now formalised through a designated training function, the school currently has a cohort of twelve trainee teachers supported by a group of highly skilled school-based mentors and coordinated by a dedicated member of staff, who is herself a former employee of Manchester Metropolitan University. As such, the school has become one of the smallest initial teacher training institutes in the country. The move to engage in teacher training has been recognised as a key step in the professional development of teachers at the school too. The reason? Quite simply that the opportunity to work as a mentor for trainee teachers forces you to reflect on your own practice in a way that is so easily lost in the hectic day to day life of a school. In the case of Matthew Moss, it also allowed colleagues to look outwards from the institution, as well as reflecting on their own practice. There, still more exciting educational approaches could be found.

'Provision for staff development is outstanding'

Ofsted report, June 2005

While many teachers tend to feel rather self-conscious at the prospect of seeing themselves on film, there have been times when staff at Matthew Moss High School have been disappointed *not* to have appeared on camera! Observation, filming and audio taping are everyday occurrences at the school. Actively encouraged by the headteacher and leadership team, a very advanced programme of professional development is in place that provides a rich interchange of expertise and good practice between colleagues. Many faculties have developed their own 'teachers' toolkits' as a result of this work—documents that inspire good practice and encourage even more creative approaches to teaching and learning. Another tool that is used to promote thoughtful reflection in the classroom is the school's *Teaching and Learning* journal, a document edited by Advanced Skills Teacher (AST) Steve Jolly.

Sharing good practice has been aided by teaching and learning newsletters at Matthew Moss High School

The student voice

I was intrigued to hear deputy head Geraldine Norman talk about her work with student observers, so I booked some time to chat with three student observers over lunch. It soon became clear that the work of the school in this area is very advanced—indeed the ability of students aged 13 and 14 to speak in a knowledgeable and passionate way about effective teaching and learning has left a lasting impression on me to this day.

Work to train the student observers began in 2005 as part of a partnership project between Matthew Moss High and Bingley Grammar School (to which a former deputy head from the school had moved that same year). Students from Matthew Moss had to apply to become student observers and participate in the training by writing a letter outlining their reasons—this ensured a talented pool of high quality and motivated students was recruited. Genuine student involvement in the training process was a key goal from the start, so it began with students watching two lessons on video and making notes on the positive and negative features of each. As student observers Nisa, Matthew and Kerry went on to describe, during the rest of the day the excitement and engaging nature of the experience became clear. The main outcome was a list of criteria to be used during lesson observations back at school that the students had decided on themselves.

Various approaches and tools were used to help students to get the best out of the day and work in a spirit of collaboration with young people from outside their friendship groups, or even from the partner school. The training day clearly allowed students to bond in a unique way and students from the two schools have kept in touch since the training day and are in the process of organising a reunion.

Teachers at all levels have benefited from the work of the student observers. Observations by students always take place in the presence of an additional teacher observer. Face to face feedback to the teacher is a critical part of the process and takes place as soon as possible after the observation. The feedback session allows the student and teacher observers to outline the strengths and weaknesses of the lesson and suggest ways it might be improved.

Intrigued to learn more about the reaction of teachers when confronted with weaknesses highlighted by year 9 student observers, I pressed repeatedly on this point. While the students admitted to feeling uncomfortable in such situations, they had clearly developed some effective strategies for making the process less painful—and more constructive—for teachers. One student spoke of mentioning the positive points first; another asking the teacher themselves to explain what had gone well and what had not worked; another of trying to make negative comments more constructive. But the student observers were clear about one point: if a lesson was not effective then the teacher needed to be told, otherwise there was no point in having student observers.

Chapter 4: Let's Focus on Learning | 115

LESSON OBSERVATION RECORD SHEET

Name of teacher		
Class	Period	
Date	Subject	
Name of Observer		

Criteria of a good lesson	Notes
Learning takes place	
Teacher has good classroom management skills and is consistent	
Teacher knows the class and communicates well with the students	
Questions are encouraged and evoked	
All students engaged and interested	
Challenging, fun and varied	
There is a range of activities	

Criteria of a good lesson	Notes
Strengths of lesson	
Points for future consideration	

Specially trained students complete lesson observation sheets to help improve standards

| We Did It Here!

> **Matthew Moss High School**
> **Humanities Faculty**
>
> [cycle diagram: CONNECT → ACTIVATE → DEMONSTRATE → CONSOLIDATE, with central "HUMANITIES and ACCELERATED L"]
>
> **Easy read Teacher Toolkit**
>
> Practical ideas for
> effective accelerated learning
> ~ tried and tested by the Humanities Team ~

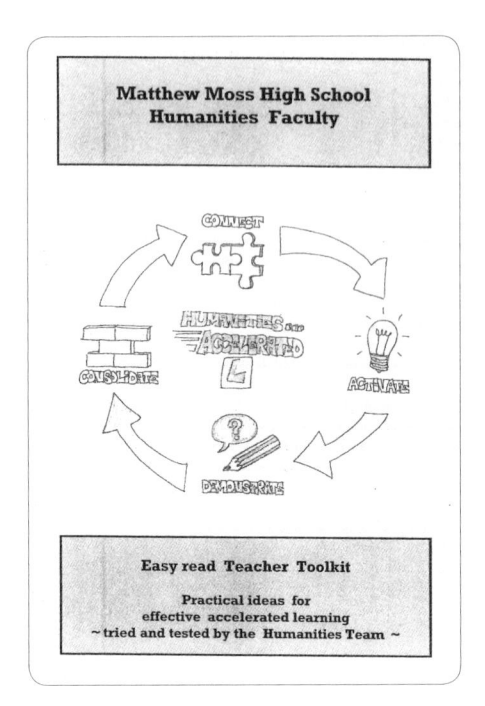

Humanities Teaching and Learning Portfolio

This portfolio is intended to be a practical guide that will help colleagues plan and provide for effective learning in History, Geography and R. E. It is in effect a Humanities Teacher Toolkit. It is based on current practice within the Humanities faculty and contains ideas developed and used by all colleagues. Moreover, this portfolio should be seen as out policy for providing, planning and developing effective practice. In putting this resource together a vote of thanks is given to all who have contributed with an extra thanks to Gill Sweet for artwork.

Included within the Toolkit are:

- Practical examples of an accelerated learning cycle
- Lesson Plans to develop short term planning and demonstrate the 4 stage learning cycle
- Suggestions and learning delineators that will help us teach to each
- Tasks that will help students recall and review learning
- Tasks that will help students recall and review learning
- Tasks that enable teachers to input new information
- Tasks that will allow students to demonstrate new learning
- An outline of the 4 learning to learn dispositions.

Steven Jolly: Head of Humanities and AST

Subject departments take responsibility for their development through a range of tools, including the humanities toolkit

I was interested to learn that the comments of the student and teacher observers on the quality of teaching and learning in lessons tend to mirror each other. A three way dialogue typifies the feedback process, with both the observers giving comments and the teacher being observed making their own responses. I was also reassured—but not surprised—to hear that the teachers being observed have responded overwhelmingly well to the process of student observation.

Steve Jolly, who has had a close involvement in the work through his role as an AST, confirmed that one of the big successes of the project has been the ability of student observers to identify the features of a good lesson. He also singled out the students' compassion for the teachers being observed too and their willingness to put across their views in a sensitive way. More recently, some of the student observers were involved in recruiting a new member of staff which required them to observe various candidates teach. It's noteworthy that the students named the same top candidate as the adult recruitment panel who had also observed the sample lessons.

The student observers have most recently been involved in making a DVD about teaching and learning at the school to be shown to all staff. This seeks to help staff understand the perceptions of students on what can be done to take things to the next level. Specifically, it seeks to encourage staff to get on more—especially in year 9 and above—with the teaching and learning rather than dwelling on the principles of Learning to Learn, which students feel are now well embedded in the higher years. The DVD is being used during a training day to stimulate staff discussions on the way ahead.

> *'Students have a high opinion of the school, and speak well of the quality of teaching and the range of extra-curricular activities that it provides. They have a positive approach to learning, and their good attitudes make a significant contribution to their academic achievement'*
>
> *Ofsted report, June 2005*

I feel the need to say at this point that if any reader has the slightest bit of scepticism about the quality of the observations made by the students on teaching and learning, I am glad to say, in this case, they are completely unfounded. This is student lesson observation and feedback of the highest order. Indeed, I can put my hand on my heart and say that the quality of the dialogue with the students about effective teaching and learning during my discussions with them—and the skill they clearly have in handling the often difficult feedback process to teachers—leads me to believe that the level of their impact on teachers clearly matches or exceeds that of *adult* observers in some other schools I've visited. What is also abundantly clear is that the student observers themselves are acquiring a whole suite of new skills that will remain with them for years to come, perhaps most significantly, the interpersonal qualities to be able to give sensitive feedback to an adult on an aspect of their professional development. The fact that so many adults have not yet mastered this skill underlines the outstanding work of the young observers at Matthew Moss.

A striking feature to emerge from my discussions with the student observers was their failure to realise how unusual and nationally significant the work they are doing is. When questioned hard on this point, it emerged that only one student had any idea that this kind of work does not happen in every school and only then because the student in question had relatives in a London school that clearly has a very different regime to the one at Matthew Moss. While they recognised that being a student observer brought many benefits to the school and themselves, and would make a fine addition to their curriculum vitae, I found their ignorance of the very special nature of their work very striking. I felt I needed to point out to them just how impressive their work was, and when I mentioned that if the Prime Minister had been in the room he would have been falling off his chair to hear how advanced their work is, the team resolutely decided to invite him to their school to hear their story face to face. All power to them I say!

An expert's views

An important feature of the work of the school, already mentioned briefly, has been the involvement of a range of expert educationalists that Andy Raymer has brought in to inspire staff. Perhaps most prominent among these in recent years is Paul Ginnis, author of the UK's best-selling handbook for teachers, *The Teacher's Toolkit*. Paul has worked with staff and students in a variety of ways since November 2004, when he first spoke about learning styles. His latest project saw a team of students produce a DVD on the quality of teaching and learning at the school. This provided an innovative means of focusing on classroom practice that came with a real sense of authenticity, as it harnessed the powerful testimonies of the students themselves.

I was interested to explore Paul's views on the achievements of the school, since he is one of the most active consultants currently supporting creative practice in UK schools, with wide experience of cutting edge work. Furthermore, Paul's most recent book has tackled the all-important area of Learning to Learn, an agenda that Matthew Moss High School has wholeheartedly embraced.

Paul spoke passionately about the impressive commitment of the school to work at the *classroom* level, which he freely admitted began many years before he first set foot in the school. He was quick to single out the key role of headteacher Andy Raymer—someone whose distinctive vision for education and natural reflectivity enabled change to take place when it might otherwise have been very slow to take root. Andy's willingness to ask big questions about *what* the school was doing and *why* it was doing those things was also identified by Paul as very significant. Paul also drew attention to the persistence and determination of Andy and Geraldine Norman, his deputy, who have stuck to their mission 'like a dog to its bone'.

A further factor singled out by Paul is the need for teachers to innovate and find effective approaches within an overall *framework* of high quality teaching and learning. While *The Teacher's Toolkit* provides a wealth of practical ideas for teachers to try, he is at pains to point out that unless teachers' work is underpinned by a deep understanding of the principles of what they're doing and why, they can soon run out of ideas. Recognising this, I was encouraged to see that many departments at Matthew Moss have fiercely customised their own teaching materials based on robust principles, as exemplified by the work of the humanities department in their own departmental 'toolkit'. In this way, the school is making important strides forward in creating a *sustainable* approach to high quality teaching and learning.

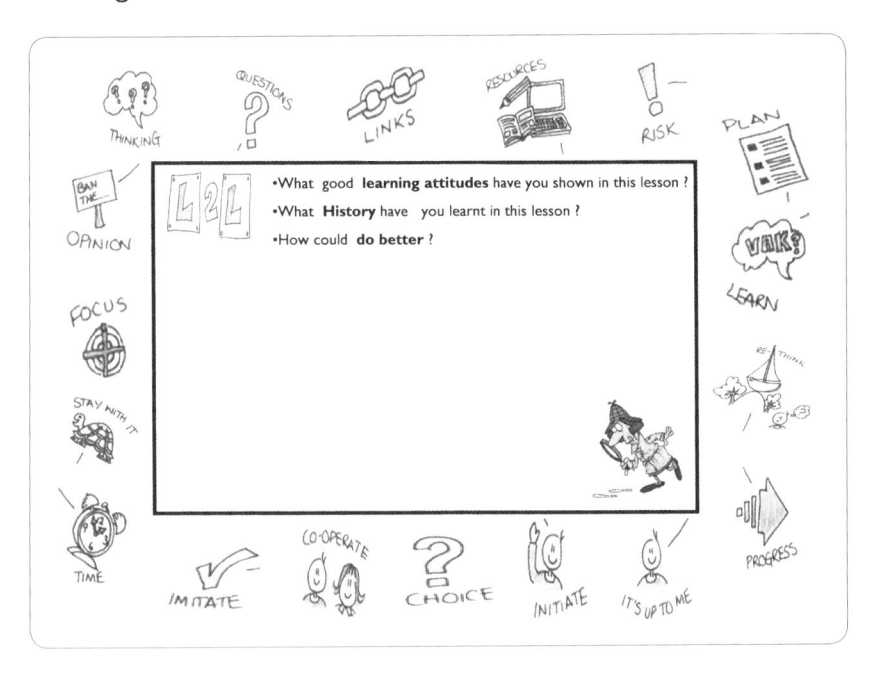

Flexibility	Stickability
Listens to others and asks others Use different resources in different situations Learn in different ways ~ uses different senses Get involved. Takes risks ~ might get it right, might get wrong	Ask questions Stay on task Overcome disruptions Ignores distractions Get back on task when stopped Get back on task when stuck Work in usual settings
Knowing me ... knowing you ...	**Learning alone .. Learning together ...**
Share ideas with others Asks as well as listens Takes part Rethinks questions and answers and ideas Knows what is to be done Knows what is expected by others	Thinks of questions to help finish task Thinks about the lesson Knows lesson objectives Works in group Works with other children Works on own Works in pairs

Flexibility – Thinking
(RESOURCES, QUESTIONS, RISK, LINKS, THINKING)

Bounce-Back-Ability + Stickability – Resilience
(FOCUS, STAY WITH IT, BAN THE OPINION, TIME)

Knowing Me Knowing You – Reflectiveness
(PLAN, RE-THINK, IMITATE, WANT 2 LEARN, PROGRESS)

Learning Together Learning Alone – Relating
(CO-OPERATE, CHOICE, IT'S UP TO ME, INITIATE)

Students are taught about the language of learning and given tools to help them develop greater confidence

Given that Paul has very wide experience of innovative practice in education I was eager to find out where he placed Matthew Moss on the spectrum of schools working to create a distinctive learning culture. He was quick to confirm that in terms of student involvement in improving teaching and learning, he had not come across a more advanced school. The school's liberal attitude to involving young people has clearly, in Paul's view, made students positive partners in improving teaching and learning.

Paul's upbeat tone about the achievements of the school, coupled with the powerful testimonies I had heard from staff and students alike, helped to paint a colourful picture of the successes of the school. As I explored the detail of that picture I began to reflect on the factors that had enabled the school to achieve its success.

The 'secrets' of success

Matthew Moss High School's success appears to have been down to a combination of at least eight interrelated factors, all of which have played important roles in the development of the school.

Focus on a core mission

The commitment of leaders and teachers at Matthew Moss High School to their core mission is deeply impressive and stands out as the principal reason for the school's success. Staff at the school are clearly united by a real passion for learning, which they bring to life through a range of imaginative approaches. The school's work to establish a distinctive language for learning and a willingness to celebrate learning in all its forms are just two manifestations of this mission. Nobody visiting the school can be in any doubt about what really *matters* in this institution. By focusing on a simple core mission the school has also been able to channel its energy into just one vital area of focus; it has also enabled it to be robust in responding to the plethora of government initiatives now influencing schools. The many conflicting demands being placed on schools can easily cause them to dilute their efforts into several disparate areas, but clearly not at Matthew Moss High School. Few schools I've visited have managed to focus their efforts so well in one essential area of their practice.

> *'Provision for staff development is outstanding'*
>
> Ofsted report, June 2005

Constancy of purpose

Learning is clearly the glue that binds the school together, but it has only been possible to focus on learning by staff going to great lengths to place emphasis on this aspect of the school at every opportunity. While this has been led by the headteacher and his deputy, important roles have been played by other key figures at the school, such as AST Steve Jolly. Such an approach requires that in staff and departmental meetings, in training sessions and in publications, the school pauses to reflect on the impact on learning before launching into any new actions.

Innovation and risk taking

There's a tangible feeling that experimentation is part of the toolkit of every teacher at Matthew Moss High School. But leaders have not just given the green light for teachers to take risks in the classroom— they've actually encouraged it. Headteacher Andy Raymer models this approach through his own experimentation and by being open to new ideas and possibilities. This helps to give other staff the 'permission' to be experimental in their own settings. I believe that schools are so much stronger where such innovation is encouraged, providing it takes place within a culture where people are not blamed for any 'failures'.

Living without fear

Another important element of the culture of the school is the supportive climate that has been created for students and staff. Andy

Raymer feels strongly that learning is only possible without fear of failure, and this works for staff as much as it does for students. While a 'no blame' culture clearly has to be tempered with accountability in any publicly funded body, this approach manifests itself through professional dialogue with staff when challenges arise, rather than over firm disciplinary procedures. Students, of course, tend to be more fragile than adults about their self-image and for them a culture that supports them, rather than blames them, is much more likely to lead to successful and happy young people.

The key role of training

The school has clearly used Continuing Professional Development (CPD) very effectively as a tool for continual improvement. Its status as one of the smallest teacher training institutions in the country is testament to the high regard it clearly has for nurturing the next generation of teachers. Lifelong learning genuinely appears to be something that matters at the school, and staff are expected to embrace this notion too through such activities at the student observation team. Expertise from within the school is also harnessed—for example, through the departmental teaching and learning handbooks which are updated on a regular basis. The school has also looked outwards to bring in expertise, inviting external experts to speak to staff and work with key departments. This commitment to training in a wide variety of forms provides the support that staff need to excel in the classroom and achieve their potential as talented teachers.

Respecting students' views—using students' skills

Use of the student voice is becoming more and more recognised by schools as a tool for improvement, but few can have embraced this notion more warmly than Matthew Moss High. Students' views are clearly respected at the school but more than that, there is a recognition that their skills and knowledge can be a powerful force for change at the school. The fact that many staff have gone on record to champion the quality of the feedback they've received from student observers in their lessons indicates that this work is clearly having an important impact at the school. By valuing the contribution of students the school is also sending out vital messages that they *matter*, helping to them to have confidence in themselves and improving the climate for learning.

Leadership

Hand in hand with the above factors comes the leadership that has been provided by Andy Raymer and his deputy Geraldine Norman. A distinctive ethos focused on learning, a commitment to risk taking and a climate without fear do not happen by accident—they become part of schools only through the carefully considered actions of leaders. Matthew Moss High School's work is clearly creative, but this brings with it risks given the current political climate which often seems to emphasise control and regimentation. It therefore requires leaders who are prepared to put their head above the parapet and stand up for what they believe in, even though compliance with government-imposed priorities may be an easier route to follow. It is to Andy's great credit that, as headteacher, he has repeatedly been prepared to stand up for what *really* matters at Matthew Moss High.

Seizing opportunities

I was eager to probe the extent to which the school's achievements had come about through meticulous planning. My assumption was that no school could create such a powerful learning culture without a well-honed strategy. So it came as something of a surprise when Andy Raymer freely admitted that the school's major successes had *not* always been planned—instead they had arisen through opportunities. These included the reorganisation of the school system in Rochdale which gave rise to Matthew Moss, the arrival of new staff with fresh ideas and the more recent training role of the school. This openness to new opportunities seems to be another distinctive part of the culture at the school; and it is made possible due to the school's work on what it calls 'strategic positioning' rather than development planning.

How transferable is this work?

We turn finally to the question of the degree to which other schools could replicate the work of Matthew Moss High School. Might the achievements of this Rochdale school be unique and untransferable?

I believe the success factors highlighted above show clearly that, although driven by visionary and inspirational leadership, a series of *targeted* actions have been carried out that have brought it closer to its goal. These are actions that other schools should be able to emulate—even if their focus is not to be so narrowly focused on learning. Constancy of purpose, a willingness to take risks and commitment to training are surely not things that are unique to a secondary school in Rochdale.

It would be unfair, however, not to single out the leadership of the school as being very significant in achieving its success. While the positive changes that the school has witnessed in the last decade *may* have eventually taken root given a less focused leadership team, there is no doubt that they would have taken considerably more time. The important message for schools from this is clear: the quality of leadership will be directly proportional to the quality of outcomes at your school.

Andy Raymer was eager to point out that being open to opportunities has really helped his school move forward. This notion is explored in a wider sense in Professor Richard Wiseman's influential book *The Luck Factor* (2004), the first scientific study of luck, which is as much a thesis on achieving success as it is a characterisation of what brings people and organisations the luck that will bring them closer to their goals. It shows us that luck is actually a state of mind and we can all develop the habits of luck to become more successful—and this works for schools too.

It's easy to become misty eyed when spending time in a school such as Matthew Moss High—an institution that inspires you through its unswerving commitment to learning in its widest sense.

Yet it is clear that what staff have created at the school is an oasis of calm, purposeful learning that is successfully inspiring young people whose lives are often far from tranquil outside the school gates. But perhaps the most important message of all is that by simplifying what schools can stand for, and by focusing on the empowering effect of learning, amazing things *are* possible. If you visit this Lancashire school, I have no doubt that you too will recognise that more than being just possible, they are also *happening* on a daily basis in this centre of excellence for teaching and learning.

> *'Many lessons involve an explanation of what is to be learnt and how it is to be learnt, often involving a discussion with the students about the importance of their learning. The range of activities is far greater than usually seen: students teaching part of the lesson, groups of fifty being made up by combining classes and then being taught by two teachers simultaneously, using signs and signals to communicate quickly how much has been understood, are all common at Matthew Moss. The emphasis is clearly upon using whatever works best. The result is lessons that students find interesting and highly enjoyable'*
>
> Ofsted report, June 2005

Chapter 5

An Enterprising School?

> 'Students need to learn how to be enterprising in order to thrive in today's changing world.' Jarvis Hayes

Spring arrived and I was three months into the research for my book. My visits to the schools featured in the previous chapters had left me feeling inspired but also a little exhausted. I needed time to take stock of what I had seen and been told. I wanted to pause and try to draw some objective conclusions about what I had witnessed, as I felt rather overwhelmed by the stories of success. As I created the space for some reflection I found that a troubling question was preying repeatedly on my mind: could I have overestimated what the schools I had visited had achieved and the relevance of this work to other schools? My fear was that I may be getting so carried away with the idea of successful schools that I had lost sight of the realities and day to day grind of school life. The need for a second opinion became more and more obvious—from somebody with real expertise in a specific aspect of education.

A chance conversation with Sophie Craven, a long-standing work colleague from my local authority advisory days in Barnsley, provided the opportunity to address these concerns head on. I had worked with Sophie on a range of enrichment projects for more able students in my role as Gifted and Talented coordinator for the authority. She was then enterprise coordinator for the Barnsley Business Education Partnership, part of a network of organisations working to promote effective educational links between schools and the world of work. Though Sophie had moved on to working in a university setting supporting the needs of schools, she remained fascinated by the factors that make schools successful. And perhaps more significantly, she possessed the analytical mind to be able to visit a school and draw objective conclusions about their successes, based on her many years of expertise in her specialist area—enterprise. This was more than convenient because I had identified the topic of enterprise in schools as a key theme that I wished to explore in the book. Fired up by the opportunity, Sophie agreed to visit a school in Cheshire where she had heard that impressive results were being obtained, based on a unique culture of enterprise. I will let Sophie tell you the story of her visit to St Nicholas Catholic High School in her own words, before returning again to make some further comments at the end of the chapter.

It was an early Friday morning when I set off across the Pennines bound for Cheshire and it felt like just another working day. I had made this journey across the M62 innumerable times, climbing to the summit and battling against the moorland elements and through streams of office workers in their cars, Manchester bound. I often set out on this route with trepidation because of the weather, but today was different: the sun was shining and spring was breathing fresh life into the moors. As I drove I pondered: I was curious as to what had made a Catholic comprehensive school somewhere in mid-Cheshire a hub of enterprise.

As I drew closer to St Nicholas Catholic High School, my thoughts turned once again to the traffic. Given the semi-rural location, the approach to the school was somewhat chaotic as buses, cars and pedestrians all made their way towards the school, channelled between the surrounding red brick houses. St Nics, as it is affectionately known, shares its grounds with a primary school, St Wilfrid's, and is situated near to Mid-Cheshire College (an FE college), making this a truly concentrated area of learning. The school is situated in the village of Hartford, with the busy market town of Northwich just two miles away.

I was meeting with Don Firkins, the enterprise manager of the school, and as I entered the building the chaos outside slipped away. The first thing I noted as unusual while I waited was the laugher that emanated from of a group of teachers who were discussing the working day ahead. Not so peculiar you may think, but many schools that I have visited during my career have an atmosphere that suggests 'We're not here to enjoy ourselves!' Then I noticed the school's mission statement on the wall and everything started to unfold—it read 'Everyone Matters'. As I was to find out during the course of the day, this mission was at the very heart of the school's success, integral to its religious doctrine but also absolutely critical to their belief in enterprise—the key focus of my visit.

The role of enterprise manager

> 'The whole thing by definition is dynamic. Everything we do leads to something else and if it's worthwhile, we'll do it!' Don Firkins

The school gained business and enterprise specialist status in September 2003 and in the same year it also gained Don Firkins. Don was recruited as an external non-teaching enterprise manager because headteacher, Gerard Boyle, recognised the need for external expertise from someone with a business background and with the drive, determination and vision to make things happen. It seems that Don was the perfect man for the job! He was a control systems engineer by profession who had a wealth of experience in business and who had worked abroad for many years, running operations in five different countries across the globe. In more recent times, before his career change, he was managing director of a local Cheshire company. So why would a semi-retired 50-something engineer want to take on such a challenge? He had, he told me 'the will to give something back to education'.

> 'The leadership of the headteacher is very good—his vision and ambition have created a school that celebrates traditional Catholic values but is also innovative in promoting an enterprise culture in the school'
>
> Ofsted report, July 2004

Don is the lifeblood of enterprise at the school. It seems he has it coursing through his veins; he lives and breathes it and, seemingly, he loves it too. Everything about Don, the way he speaks, what he says, his body language, makes him the beating heart of enterprise at St Nics. Don admits that, at first, he wasn't fit for purpose. He didn't understand the school system and in order for him to be effective and gain credibility he had to learn fast. Now he understands 'the system' he is able to bring his wealth of business experience to bear.

Currently in its fourth year as a Business and Enterprise College (BEC), I was intrigued by the school's approach to enterprise. During my discussions with staff at the school the word *inclusive* was used time and time again. The school has a broad definition of enterprise, and certainly the main emphasis here is on enterprise rather than business, because it encompasses so much more and is therefore more inclusive.

The essence of enterprise at St Nicholas

School mission statement

'We aspire to embrace the Gospel and its values, celebrating uniqueness and diversity. Our learning, within an enterprise culture, is based upon trust and respect which define our relationships with the world family. Everyone matters.'

Beyond the school's general mission statement, Don admits that the vision for enterprise was cloudy to start with, or rather they knew the future they wanted to create, but how they were going to get there was much less certain.

As Don puts it: 'Schools like to exist in an environment of certainty. The problem with enterprise is that by its very nature it doesn't give you certainty or absolutes. Enterprise is about a journey, but there isn't one direction. Actually there isn't even a finishing point! Things can always be developed, improved and taken further to the next level. By its very nature the development of the whole thing is very organic.'

Business and Enterprise College mission statement

'Develop in our students the capability to handle uncertainty and respond positively to change; to create and implement new ideas and new ways of doing things, to make reasonable risk/reward assessments and act upon them in school and into their personal and working lives.'

As a business the school will be permeated by a growing appreciation of the increasingly global nature of society, and business in particular; students will explore issues of economic interdependence in partnership with our community partners and sponsors. As an 'Enterprise College' St Nicholas seeks to embrace the challenge and opportunities presented by the evolving global, national and local economies, for the benefit of its students and the wider community by improving the quality of teaching and learning across all areas of the curriculum, and in particular in business studies, ICT, maths and modern foreign languages.

The school will contribute to improving the quality of life and enhancing the range of economic opportunity available to those who have retired, the young disabled and the young unemployed locally. This involvement of minority and disadvantaged groups will facilitate their inclusion in lifelong learning and wealth creating opportunities.

Students will continue to extend their understanding of the nature of their wider social responsibilities. They will encounter the moral and ethical dimensions inherent in economic decision-making processes and have the opportunity to exercise their judgement, both in relation to 'real' world case studies and activities designed for the purpose.

Through the influence of our own School Eco Group and other organisations, matters of sustainability, creative regeneration and healthy living will be addressed across the school community.

The school will encourage the development of self-confidence, creativity, flexibility and adaptability in all its stakeholders. Our young people will be challenged to develop their understanding of what it means to be a consumer, a producer, an entrepreneur and an adviser in the dynamic enterprise culture of the twenty-first century. The development of a strong ethos of entrepreneurial and business acumen will enhance student attainment across the curriculum and encourage the study of new technologies and their application.

The specialist subject areas of business education, ICT, mathematics and modern foreign languages will be a focus for the acquisition of a wider range of skills including teamworking, mind-friendly learning, evaluation techniques, decision-making processes, problem-solving, communication and working within a culture of deadlines. The school will improve the levels of attainment of students within these specialist areas and extend the range of related extra-curricular activities; in doing so the number of students engaged in these areas of the curriculum will be increased.

The school will facilitate an increased access to facilities and expertise with our community partners. The promotion and sharing of good professional practice will be a feature of our links with them, as will our commitment to being an inclusive community.

We intend to be a more dynamic, higher achieving community; our increased emphasis on improving the quality of learning in our school, blended with a business and enterprise culture, will transform our role in the community, so that we can offer proof positive that we are committed to all the principles of specialist schools. St Nicholas Catholic High School unashamedly strives to be a world-class school; business enterprise specialist status is helping us get there.

'The gaining of business and enterprise specialist status and the commitment to raising an awareness of enterprise meets the needs of students in the twenty-first century extremely well'

Ofsted report, July 2004

Despite the stated lack of clarity on the actions needed to achieve the vision, it is self-evident that the sheer determination and passion for the enterprise cause has been enough to propel the school towards a better future. Indeed, one might think that the school's business and enterprise mission statement, which in parts can almost be likened to a political speech, is just a collection of carefully chosen buzzwords—but not so. I was utterly convinced that these words are being transformed into reality at this school, as the case studies and examples that follow will show.

To Don, the essence of enterprise can be summed up in the following way:

- Enterprise is Attitude not ability
- Enterprise is Skills not knowledge
- Enterprise is Culture not rules
  (Reed International)

To my mind this is an unusual and somewhat brave supposition, given that the foundations of most schools are built upon ability, knowledge and rules.

Tell me, I forget

Show me, I remember
Involve me, I understand
Let me try and fail then I may
learn and ultimately succeed.

Enterprise proverb, Don Firkins

Work-related Learning and Enterprise Policy (2005)

Effective enterprise learning takes place in an *environment* —a school, a community or business setting—where young people are given autonomy to tackle relevant problems or issues that involve an element of risk and uncertainty about final outcomes, as well as reward for their successful resolution.

Learners are expected to take personal responsibility for their own actions through an enterprise process that involves four stages.

Stage 1 – Tackling a problem or need

Students generate ideas through discussion to reach a common understanding of what is required to resolve the problem or meet the need.

Stage 2 – Planning the project or activity

Breaking down tasks, organising resources, deploying team members, allocating responsibilities.

Stage 3 – Implementing the plan

Solving problems, monitoring progress.

Stage 4 – Evaluating the processes

Reviewing the activities and final outcomes, reflecting on lessons learned and assessing the skills, attitudes, qualities and understanding acquired.

In the early days—why enterprise?

I was intrigued to know how the enterprise culture at St Nics had first become established. Don told me that in the early days before BEC status, 'the school was running with the notion without really giving it a name'. I was eager to find out what had motivated such an 'academic' school (seventy-nine to eighty-one per cent GCSE A*– C pass rate in recent years, with contextual value added scores from Key Stage 2 to 3 placing it in the top ten per cent of schools in the country) to opt for business and enterprise as a specialism in preference to something more traditional: modern foreign languages or science, for instance. I also wondered how business and enterprise sat with the school's Catholic faith. Once again, the notion of inclusion was the driving force. It was felt that enterprise was the ideal vehicle for incorporating all departments in the school; other specialisms were viewed as less inclusive for the whole. And here's how enterprise and Catholicism can coexist: through the notion of inclusion, where, as the school's mission states, 'everybody matters' and nobody 'in the family' is excluded. (It's certainly noteworthy that the school's motto of 'Everyone Matters' was coined well before the national Every Child Matters agenda.)

Once Don was on board, his drive and passion for enterprise was fuelled by much grander concerns: the need to raise the skill level of the workforce, which is central to improving the nation's competitiveness in an ever-changing global economy. For Don this is at the heart of the need for a culture change, not only in this school, but in every school across the land. This is why Don prefers the concept of enterprise to business, as for him it is so much more than business start-up. It's about, as Don puts it: 'Instilling a culture where students take personal responsibility for their lives and careers' (whether that is in 'business' in the traditional sense or not).

St Nics is different in many respects to other business and enterprise schools. In the early days Don visited other BEC schools and found, at that time at least, that the majority had very different profiles to his own. Many of the others were struggling and, where formal education wasn't working, were using enterprise to try to move forward and improve. 'Whilst other schools were using it as their salvation, we wanted to use it to build on our success and achievement,' admits Don.

Of course this created its own unique set of problems. It's much more difficult to persuade people of the need to do things differently and change when you are already successful. Don quickly recognised that the timetable for formal lessons at the school was heavily protected and guarded and, as a result, things needed to be built slowly and quietly. The school had to be very careful and conservative in moving forward. In these early days the school held one or two enterprise days, although interestingly, they were not overtly labelled as such.

Other key ambassadors

During my visit to the school I also met Angela Norman, assistant headteacher with responsibility for the BEC specialism, and head of business studies and ICT. She exuded energy and sheer passion for teaching, the like of which I have rarely before seen. What's more, Angela and Don clearly fed off each other's enthusiasm and during our time together the room buzzed from the energy levels within.

> 'We are a very proactive school—we have high standards already but always strive to do better. We are always trying to incorporate new and innovative ideas.' Don Firkins

The decision to opt for business and enterprise as a specialism was made in close consultation with all staff but at that time one relatively new member of staff to the school was particularly supportive of the idea. Angela entered teaching as a business studies teacher in 1999 at the age of 36, with a previous career in insurance and motherhood. Angela's passion for teaching was self-evident; she cares wholeheartedly about the children in this school and gives them 100 per cent of her time, energy and enthusiasm.

Back then the business studies department was already innovative, in terms of its non-traditional approach to teaching. 'In order to teach the subject effectively there is a need for real life input,' Angela explains. Business studies was the first area in which such an academic school offered vocational courses. 'For us this was quite revolutionary!' she admits. The school now offers a range of vocational qualifications including the NFTE (National Foundation for Teaching Entrepreneurship), Applied GCSEs and Applied A-levels in IT and Business. The school also offers Law A-level too. 'We don't want to be labelled academic or vocational', she maintains, 'but rather have a complementary blend and a mixture.' Again, I hear the word *inclusive* mentioned.

There's also been a development from 'traditional' teaching to more experimental methods in the department, pioneered by Angela. She tells me for example that she often sets her class up to represent the organisational structure of a business, giving different roles within the structure to her students. This way they learn more effectively than studying a diagram in a textbook by doing it in an enterprising and hands-on way. To some teachers this method of teaching is probably considered dangerous because of 'what could go wrong', but Angela strikes me (like Don) as someone who's happy to experiment, change things around and take chances. And, I ask myself, isn't this what enterprise and being enterprising is all about? As Don outlines later in the day, 'Enterprise starts with innovation in teaching.'

As part of GCSE Business Angela also uses sixth form drama students who act, in character, as applicants for a job. Students then have to decide who they would offer the job to, justifying their decisions. The department also makes use of Profitable Pursuits at advanced level (a computer business simulation developed by Rolls Royce) and the Business Game from Pixel Learning (a virtual company) at Key Stage 4. As Don points out, 'Everything you do in business has an effect, and these games teach our students this important lesson which can be applied in all aspects of our lives.' The games are used as a kind of reward system in the classroom, but also serve to reinforce and contextualise the business studies learning.

The school has a business suite that is described as a 'classroom of the twenty-first century'. It looks to me at first glance like a company boardroom rather than a classroom and in many respects this is exactly what it is. The room has been designated 'special use'. It is not timetabled but rather bookable—although it can't be used for traditional classroom activity.

Embedding enterprise into the curriculum and classroom

To illustrate the range of work taking place to make enterprise a key part of the culture at St Nics, I will draw attention in the next section to various examples of work that have been undertaken at the classroom and whole school level.

External speakers programme

Given the protection of the cornerstone timetable, in year one of specialist school status Don introduced a programme of guest speakers into the classroom. The idea was to make the environment more real, interesting, inspiring, unique and enterprising whilst not eroding the traditional timetable. Very quickly the school went from a few speakers to about fifty or sixty per year. Don has tried to map presenters on to the curriculum and make them 'fit for purpose', so that the speaker becomes part of the lesson and not just a bolt-on in order to tick a 'business intervention' box. Don spends time with speakers planning their presentation against the objectives for the lesson and how it fits into the scheme of work. Don refers to this process as 'fine-tuning speakers to fit into the curriculum'. For me this was a revelation. As a coordinator at an education business partnership, I struggled for many years to persuade schools to dedicate this necessary time to fine-tuning. As a result, many of the school–business partnerships that I helped establish were not successful and relationships floundered because neither party really got what they wanted from the deal. As Don puts it, 'The holy grail is weaving it into the scheme of work.'

Speakers were invited from a wide range of areas, including the public and private sector. Some examples include Chester Law College, M&S Money, United Biscuits, Jaguar Cars, Alton Towers, JCB and a range of universities including Manchester, Leeds, Lancaster, Chester and Salford.

Although the programme of speakers was a great success, Don is constantly asking himself, 'How can we make things better?' In response to his question Don built on the programme of speakers in the second year by introducing another dimension—problem-solving. Speakers were asked to provide real examples of problems facing their company or organisation and leave challenges for students to solve. Some companies added yet another layer by offering prizes to those who came up with the best solutions. The programme of guest speakers continues and I am in no doubt that it will be built upon and enhanced further.

Classroom discourse: enterprise learning

In addition to the external speakers programme, all staff are required to embed enterprise into their schemes of work and into their lessons. The physical proof of this is evident in every classroom around the school, because on the wall at the front of each room there's a large poster displaying enterprise skills and capabilities. Enterprise is clearly part of the school's discourse at classroom level between staff and students and these helpful charts serve as a visual reminder to prompt discussions on the enterprise 'learning' that has taken place in each lesson, whatever the subject area.

Students in every lesson at St Nics are are asked to consider the enterprise skills they have learnt

Schemes of work and lesson planning

During my visit I also met with Steve Turnbull, a design technology (DT) teacher, who had really bought in to the notion of enterprise as a vehicle for more effective teaching and learning. As a result of this belief, Steve had joined the school's Enterprise Group about eighteen months previously and since then has been working hard to really develop the links between enterprise and his subject. Steve told me that he recognised that there were elements of DT that should have had an enterprise focus but which weren't being addressed. 'Teamwork, problem-solving and initiative are all enterprise skills used by DT students,' he recognised. Steve then quoted me an interesting statement made by educationalist Richard Kimble, which to him epitomises the creative freedom required to teach DT: 'The best DT lesson is taught on the edge of chaos.'

The school has introduced an enterprise capability matrix which is being used and mapped against schemes of work. Steve shows me an example of one for year 10 graphics and then shows me how enterprise, and the language of enterprise, is being embedded into his lesson planning. It demonstrates the strategic way in which some departments are treating the development of enterprise skills within specific subject areas.

Key Stage 4 Enterprise Capability Skills Matrix

shaded areas indicate where skills are being taught and used within each project

The matrix columns (EC1–EC16) correspond to the following skills:
- EC1: External Agency / Organisation
- EC2: Using Initiative
- EC3: Making decisions or choices
- EC4: Making presentations
- EC5: Working in a team
- EC6: Building self confidence
- EC7: Being open-minded / divergent thinking
- EC8: Organising people
- EC9: Persuading others
- EC10: Demonstrating innovation, risk & change
- EC11: Improvising and adapting
- EC12: Responding positively to change
- EC13: Using problem solving skills
- EC14: Demonstrating project management
- EC15: Being creative / showing new ideas
- EC16: Being a leader

Year 10 - Graphics
- Term 1.1 - Skills development
- Term 1.2 - PrintIT challenge
- Term 2.1 - Christmas Project
- Term 2.2 - Christmas Project & CAD Skills
- Term 3.1 - GCSE Game coursework
- Term 3.2 - GCSE Game Coursework

Year 11 - Graphics
- Term 1.1 - GCSE Game coursework
- Term 1.2 - GCSE Game coursework
- Term 2.1 - GCSE Game coursework
- Term 2.2 - Skills & Revision
- Term 3.1 - Skills & Revision

Additional: During the course of year 10 pupils will often be given the opportunity to design and manufacture the promotional material for the school production and to enter any other design competitions that arise. A visit is usually organised for them to go to a Print Company also.

Enterprise matrices help embed topics into specific subject areas

Key Stage 3 student passport

In addition to embedding enterprise into schemes of work, lesson planning and day to day teaching, the school has also developed a cross-curricular scheme linking and weaving enterprise in with other strands such as Personal, Social and Health Education (PSHE), citizenship, work-related learning and careers education. This has been achieved through the creation of what the school calls a Key Stage 3 'student passport'. As Steve Turnbull tells me, 'One of the key challenges with enterprise is documenting that you've done it and then getting students to recognise that they've done it —that enterprise has been part of their learning.' The passport helps with this and enables students to make the connections with the enterprise in their lessons. The passport is still in its infancy, and as Steve admits, is in need of further development and improvement. Judging by the school's perseverance in other areas I am in no doubt that they will continue to fine-tune and hone the scheme until it's truly embedded and utilised across the school.

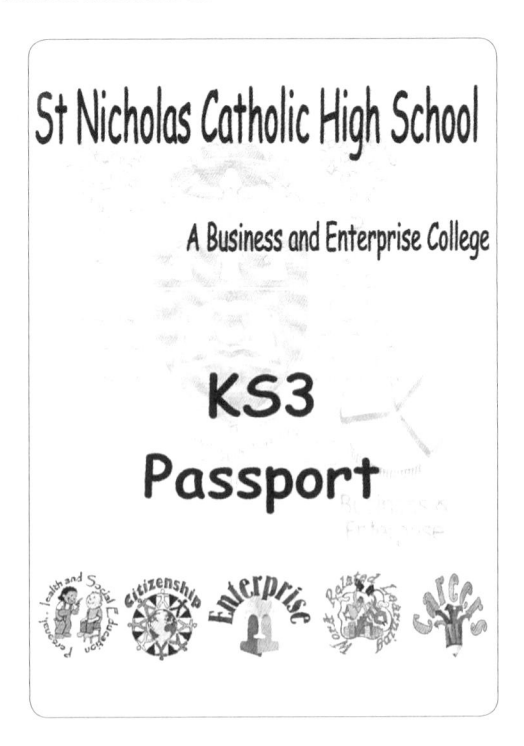

St Nicholas Catholic High School

A Business and Enterprise College

KS3 Passport

Skills

Learning Outcomes	Subject Area	When I did it (subject & date)
Reflect on and assess your strengths in relation to personality, work and leisure	P, Ca, W	
Develop effective ways of resisting pressures which threatens your personal safety and wellbeing or involves doing wrong including knowing when and where to get help and to recognise when others need help and how to support them	P	
Communicate confidently with your peers and adults.	P	
Know how and where to find information and advice about topical political, spiritual, moral, social and cultural issues, problems and events	P	
Analyse information and its sources, including ICT based sources to research e.g. the risks of early sexual activity, drug misuse, self-defence, community issues e.g. recycling, bullying etc	P,C	
Develop relationships eg by working together in a range of groups and social settings with your peers and others		
by being responsible for a mini enterprise scheme as part of a small group eg mini market		

Students are given special passports that show how specific skills will be developed

'Good links are being built with industry and within the business enterprise culture of the school'

Ofsted report, July 2004

Enterprise groups and businesses

The school has encouraged and supported the establishment of several enterprise groups and companies. For example, Steve Turnbull has supported a Key Stage 3 enterprise group—EnTech; their only brief is 'To use design to be enterprising'. So far the small group of students from year 7 to 9 has developed Christmas cards using a copper enamelling process, Valentine's Day key rings and Easter chocolates using plastic moulds. Each time the students sell the goods within school and then reinvest the profits into their next venture.

Other businesses around school include Little Cooks, V-DEC and Vintage. Little Cooks was formed by a group of year 10 students who cater for different events within the school. The company has been operating for just over a year and all profits are fed back into the company. Vintage is a company originally started through the Young Enterprise scheme, consisting of ten dedicated sixth form students. V-DEC (Victorious, Dynamic, Enterprise Corporation) is a company operated by sixth form students who produce printed T-shirts, mouse mats, mugs and caps. They can produce high quality merchandise quickly and at reasonable prices. V-DEC has operated to produce goods for a number of external companies, often producing them at a more competitive price than other manufacturers.

The Stock Market Challenge

During the Stock Market Challenge all 120 year 12 students operate in groups with £100,000 to invest in the FTSE 100, during what is effectively 'five weeks of the world'. The groups compete, round by round, to increase the value of their pseudo investment trusts.

To make the whole day realistic the school uses only real companies as listed in the FTSE 100; they use real current share values each 'week' and video-based news stories written within school and recorded professionally by nationally recognised newsreaders. The day starts and finishes with a live link to the London stock market through video-conferencing, increasing the reality of the challenge as a whole. It is certainly significant that the challenge, which takes place on the last day of the school year, is missed by nobody.

> *'Teachers and students benefit from a high quality business environment in which to work and there are measurable gains in the quality of students' work as a result of increased business links and the ready availability of ICT resources'*
>
> Ofsted report, July 2004

One Water campaign

One project which particularly interested me, and which emphasised the school's commitment to social and ethical enterprise, was the One Water campaign. The project was launched in school assembly by founder of One Water, Duncan Goose. The launch set the students off on a journey to pursue a One Water campaign to raise funds for the development of water pumps for impoverished parts of Africa. One Water mineral water was sold during enterprise week to support charitable causes.

The One Water project epitomised the school's social conscience around enterprise—that of being creative to help others or, as Don puts it, 'Thinking of new ways of doing things for the benefit of the community.' Don talks about the power to change and make a difference: 'What business entrepreneurs are to the economy, social entrepreneurs are to social change. They are the driven, creative individuals who question the status quo, exploit new opportunities, refuse to give up, and remake the world for the better.' This emphasis on social enterprise is all bound up with the school's religious foundations, and the two notions coexist very happily within the context of 'the world family'.

Rewards for innovation

Two schemes have been launched that have proved to be a real motivational influence on students and a reward for success and achievement. First is the Enterprise Reward Scheme, by which students who use their initiative at school and demonstrate an enterprising idea or activity can be rewarded in a variety of ways, from complimentary lunch vouchers to business lunches in the business suite for a whole group. This is all part of motivating the students to think and exercise enterprise more readily. Schoolthink, on the other hand, is a creative ideas website, which is similar to an organisation's employee 'suggestion scheme'. Students are encouraged as part of this scheme to think about how they might improve aspects of the school, which may benefit the school and others. The ideas are judged outside of the school and cash prizes are available every month.

INSET for staff

Probably one of the greatest challenges for the school was to get staff on board with enterprise and also to make them, as much as the students, more enterprising. Don is concerned that many teachers don't perceive that the world outside of school has changed and is changing. If they don't believe that the world has changed then why should they see the need to change themselves? To give them a practical insight into the modern workplace in 2006 the school set up the Staff into Business Programme, where every member of teaching staff (sixty-five in total) underwent a business placement. This was organised in conjunction with the local Connexions service and Education Business Partnership. It was received in a mixed fashion, which ironically served to highlight the fact that many staff would be resistant to change. However, staff gained a great deal from the experience and notably a few dissenters even had a change of heart.

In addition, Don runs INSET on enterprise for the local authority in Cheshire. Interestingly the INSET is welcomed and well received by schools who recognise the need for change, but not always by teachers who are reluctant to change. For Don this may be an uphill battle, but one which is worth the fight. He seems determined to spread the message on the importance of enterprise education and I doubt that teachers' reluctance to change will stand in his way!

Enterprise and Education Alliance

As part of its BEC responsibilities the school is leading the way in the development of enterprise in the region. In order to continue to make progress the school offers 'consultancy' to other Cheshire schools and, as part of the development, has helped form the Enterprise Education Alliance (EEA).

Don proactively seeks out 'products' and packages for the school to buy into, but what he found was that they tended to be business focused. Ever entrepreneurial, he recognised a gap in the market and set up the EEA in conjunction with local training company Lanyard Partnership Ltd. This is a private, not-for-profit organisation which helps the school to meet the needs of the local community. The alliance offers training for schools and a range of activity days for students on private enterprise and entrepreneurship, corporate enterprise, social enterprise and public sector enterprise. Workshops cover topics such as creativity and innovation, ethical trading, problem-solving, initiative and resourcefulness, the stock market and social awareness.

What has the school achieved?

The case studies above illustrate the impressive array of initiatives currently under way in the school that are helping to create a centre of excellence for enterprise at this Cheshire school. The success of the school can, however, be judged in other ways. One is the respect it has gained from other schools. In February 2007 it was invited to deliver a presentation at the annual National Conference of Business and Enterprise Colleges. At the conference staff highlighted the school's starting position, the journey travelled, key milestones along the way and its achievements to date (see below). Students from the school also attended to present a virtual tour of the school and to showcase some of the enterprising learning that is taking place.

> ### Progress in a nutshell
>
> *BEC starting position*
>
> - Very high-performing school
> - Business studies the only enterprising 'light'
> - Minimum 'collapsed timetable' days
> - Few external agencies in school
> - Charitable by nature—faith school
> - No community plan
>
> *The journey*
>
> - Staff INSET—win hearts and minds
> - Timetable planning and scheduling
> - Senior management team support in development

- Whole staff work-based placement
- Build year on year (we are never satisfied!)
- Pilot new ideas and then embed them
- Explore and take chances
- Support local authority in consulting with other schools
- Develop partnerships

Key milestones on the journey

- Enterprise coordinator appointed
- CPD programme for enterprise
- ICT classroom facilitator
- Embedding the enterprise culture
- Introduction of social enterprise

BEC overview (four years on)

- More than fifty guest speakers per year (11,000 student hours)
- Multi subject reach
- Enterprise team established (staff)
- Enterprise days for each year group (one to two per year group, fifty per cent in-house)
- Enterprise week, single theme and week-long activity
- Regular community activity
- Results still improving
- Enterprise content established in schemes of work and lesson plans
- Cross-curricular enterprise
- Key Stage 3 student passport launched
- Host special needs school enterprise days
- Active Spoke (already held CPD)
- Teaching and learning—common focus in each classroom on enterprise skills
- School newspaper launch (editorial team from year 12 with input from whole school)

- Primary school enterprise days
- EnTech—Key Stage 3 enterprise group established (years 7–9)
- A number of school businesses set up by students (e.g. Little Cooks, V-DEC and Vintage)

There have been many challenges along the way. For Don, the major challenges have been around getting staff on board, staff use of ICT, planning enterprise into schemes of work and getting students to recognise the enterprise skills they are developing. Ever the persistent optimist, challenges don't appear to dampen his spirits and Don appears to have the energy to press on and meet these challenges head on.

Measuring success

The school has evidently come a long way in four years, but I was keen to find out how it measures success. The focus is on the three key areas of staff, students and improving standards.

Teachers are a very sceptical breed. As Don puts it, 'If what we do doesn't add value then many teachers won't do it again. It's as simple as that. The fact that more and more people are buying into enterprise and it's becoming more of a whole school thing is certainly one measure of our success.'

Staff comments

'The carefully constructed use of guest speakers and site visits has substantially improved the levels of attainment for our GCSE and A-level students across many subjects.'

> 'Enterprise, particularly social enterprise, has added a completely new dimension to school life; the annual celebration of National Enterprise Week in November is particularly memorable as it involves the whole school for the week.'

The enthusiasm of students about enterprise and their school in general is certainly a demonstration of success. Students seem to be truly engaged with their learning in an enterprise context.

Student comments

> 'On enterprise you never know what's going to happen next.'

> 'The visitors to the classroom bring the subject to life, and can answer all our questions.'

> 'The interactive business simulators we use in lessons really spur us on as they're used as a reward for our efforts; they also reveal just how competitive business really is.'

When asked what enterprise skills they have developed as part of their DT work at Key Stage 4, a group of students had no problem identifying the five key areas of problem-solving, coming up with ideas in a timescale, using your initiative, time management and keeping to deadlines. This is clearly a school where young people are confident talking about enterprise and how it relates to their learning.

> 'Business education makes a significant contribution to the development of key skills. As a result, business students demonstrate a high degree of confidence and maturity'
>
> Ofsted report, July 2004

It makes sense that this 'buy in' and enthusiasm for enterprise, from staff and students alike, would lead to improvements in grades and achievement at all levels. For the real high achievers enterprise has added an extra dimension of stretch and challenge, and for those less able or disaffected with school, enterprise offers them a sense of real hope.

Although the school hasn't necessarily been placed in the enterprise limelight, Don is very aware of the significance of their work. He is involved in the enterprise agenda across the Cheshire area, providing INSET and also working with the Enterprise and Education Alliance. The school has also received interest at a national level through the National Enterprise Network. Locally, the school has a great deal of community involvement, including work with feeder primary schools, secondary schools, the wider community—including the University of the Third Age—local charities and the business community (new small businesses are encouraged to use the school's facilities free of charge to help them get established).

The work the school is doing is showcased and celebrated in a variety of ways, both internally and externally. The methods include letters to parents, the headteacher's newsletter, liaison with local press, the recently established school newspaper, and communication with the National Enterprise Network and the Specialist School Trust.

> 'The school's specialist status as a business and enterprise college has enhanced community links'
>
> Ofsted report, July 2004

A vision for the future

Don's vision for the future is to continue to make sure that the school's enterprise work is up to date, relevant and deals with current affairs. He aims to fine-tune what has already been achieved and then build on that year on year. It seems there's no time to sit still or rest here. For instance, Don tells me he would like to introduce some pilot sessions for students to supplement the curriculum on themes such as project management and planning. I am in no doubt that it will happen, along with many more new and exciting initiatives.

In short, what Don is striving for is the complete integration of enterprise in all subjects, in all lessons, in all key stages, such that it's effected naturally and becomes second nature in the classroom. The enterprise challenge days will then become celebrations of the school's collective enterprise achievements rather than the school's main provision of enterprise education. 'We have got to start delivering it by nature and not by edict,' he says. I am convinced that this is by no means the last word on enterprise for Don or for St Nics.

> *'Strategic planning is good; this is reflected in the development plans to promote an enterprise culture'*
>
> Ofsted report, July 2004

The 'secrets' of success

Having established the innovative nature of the enterprise work taking place at the school I wanted to explore what it sees as the secrets of its success to date. For Don there are at least four key factors that have been instrumental.

Building and maintaining external relationships

At the start it was difficult to develop links with business on the scale required. Not one to be deterred, Don set about writing to all of the students' parents with a proforma requesting support for the school.

Initially the school's leaders took some persuading on this somewhat irregular use of parents, but nevertheless he got the go-ahead to try something new. The request to parents was made on a very personal level, in what struck me as a Lord Kitchener-like call to arms: 'Do you want to help your child?' Out of 800 letters Don had less than fifty responses, and of those the school has built lasting relationships with about thirty parents as sustainable business contacts. For Don, the key to maintaining such relationships is to treat people professionally; after all he has himself been on the other side of the fence. For each intervention Don writes a confirmation letter, ensures someone is there to meet and greet the visitor on arrival at the school and even has their name displayed on the visitor board. He also meets them prior to the session to go through preparation and afterwards gives them feedback time, followed up by a thank you letter. Don tells me that lots of companies will help you if you help them to help you: 'All business speakers want is for students to be receptive—and they are here because we have worked hard to make the speakers' sessions relevant to the curriculum.' He goes on to add that poor communication is one of the reasons that relationships between schools and businesses fail. Most businesses, if they could reliably communicate effectively with schools, would welcome the opportunity of working with them.

Securing funding

The funding that has come with specialist school status has enabled St Nics to be 'enterprising'. It has funded a dedicated post for the school's enterprise champion—Don. It has also paid for vital infrastructure, primarily ICT, which has proved essential to the progress of the school. When Don joined the school he felt that there wasn't enough innovation and change in the classroom. There certainly wasn't enough technology. The funding which specialist status has brought with it has helped to update the ICT infrastructure in the school. This has included the installation of video conferencing equipment, interactive whiteboards, more PCs with up-to-date software and a state-of-the-art business suite. Don assumed that the new equipment would be utilised immediately but quickly found that it was much underused. The main problem was lack of confidence amongst staff who were used to more traditional teaching methods. The introduction of ICT also meant that people would have to adapt their schemes of work and that would mean extra work and, probably most frightening of all, new and unfamiliar approaches. In response to this problem, the school created a new role of ICT classroom facilitator and this has been one of the great successes so far. The school has also invested in appropriate equipment to allow enterprise projects where students can produce high quality and saleable goods, for example, printing memorabilia, presses for caps, mugs, T-shirts and mouse mats. This equipment is the basis of school businesses like V-DEC.

Forward planning and timetabling

Planning is singled out as a very significant factor that has allowed the school to put enterprise firmly on the agenda. Every enterprise initiative is planned in the previous year as it is impossible to fit anything in on the run—for example, guest speakers' outline slots are identified in the previous year's planning, as are day events and visits and trips out of school.

The roles of individuals and groups

The role of individuals and groups cannot be understated. At St Nics an Enterprise Team has been created to ensure that there is a 'group' to lead, drive and direct, to take key decisions and to make things happen. The group and the whole enterprise agenda receive strong support from the school leadership team, including the headteacher and senior leaders. While enterprise is increasingly becoming a shared vision across the school there's still a need for people with clearly defined roles and responsibilities to pioneer new ideas and make things happen. It's particularly important that the school has a dedicated enterprise manager, and probably most significant that he is not a member of teaching staff. Overall it is the determination, hard work, perseverance and enthusiasm of these dedicated staff members, complemented by a visionary person with the time and the belief to make things happen, that seem to be the recipe for success at this outstanding Cheshire school.

> 'Invest time. I can't tell you how much time you have to invest to break the barrier.' Don Firkins

Don's advice for success

- Enterprise starts with innovation in teaching
- Enterprise needs ICT as a 'catalyst'
- Appoint an ICT classroom facilitator
- Encourage links with external organisations
- Establish inter-subject links/projects
- Enterprise agenda needs leadership
- An Enterprise Group (critical mass) is essential
- Ask how do you know enterprise is in a school's genes? Check the school DNA—Dynamic, Natural, Attitude

How transferable is this work?

Finally, we turn to the extent to which the work of St Nics could be replicated in other schools. Overall I feel that there's nothing unique here—no special privileges, no lessons that cannot be learnt and replicated elsewhere. There's much at St Nics that other schools could use to emulate success in their own institutions. To my mind there are several factors that have influenced the 'good fortunes' of this school. Interestingly, I didn't have to work hard to seek out the secrets of their success—these factors were discussed openly throughout the course of my visit. In the first instance, it seems that how you *channel* the resources at your disposal is a key factor. At this school, much of the resources were channelled into ICT infrastructure which has made a dramatic impact on the quality of teaching and learning facilities.

Human resources were also considered paramount—namely in the form of the enterprise manager post. The school recognised the need for a dedicated person to drive the enterprise agenda forward and to really make things happen. The decision to appoint a non-teaching member of staff with a background from outside the education system was one made with foresight and vision.

This investment also led on to another success factor—the importance of individuals. I have no doubt that much of what has been achieved at St Nics is down to the sheer determination, hard work, enthusiasm and conviction of staff at the school—perhaps most notably, Don Firkins. However, the environment or ethos of the school is also worthy of mention—a culture where everyone matters, where everyone is nurtured as part of the 'family' and where hard work, creativity and excellence are rewarded. Such is the prevailing culture at this school that it has allowed staff to achieve their vision, both as individuals and collectively.

Sophie's comprehensive account on her visit paints a fascinating picture of life at St Nicholas Catholic High School. While the work of the school has clearly left a deep impression on her, she has also placed on record that she considers its efforts can be replicated in other schools—if they learn the lessons from this innovative school. What Sophie has also helped to show here is that the journey to success for schools can be very challenging, and that it needs determination and conviction to see things through.

I want to end this chapter by drawing attention to an important principle that I feel the work of St Nicholas Catholic High School illustrates—namely that schools that are *already* deemed to be successful in some areas can build on this to yield even greater success. The spirit of continuous improvement, regardless of the starting point, is demonstrated so well by the work of Don Firkins and his team, and there are key messages here for all schools.

Buoyed up by Sophie's findings on enterprise from this Cheshire school, I began to think more deeply about the potential for schools to work with external partners more systematically. Aware that many schools are now linking up with other institutions to tackle local priorities together, I realised that a case study of such a collaboration—and the success it has brought—could be a valuable addition to the book. Soon I was heading for an old haunt of mine in South Yorkshire where I knew there was a partnership that fitted the bill perfectly.

> 'A climate of innovation, challenge, support and improvement has been successfully created'
>
> Ofsted report, July 2004

Chapter 6

Regenerating Education through Partnership

> 'Though I'm the project manager and company secretary, I don't like the limelight—I prefer to let the schools gain the publicity they deserve.' Julianne Duffy

The first decade of the twenty-first century will be remembered as a time when schools joined together in new and exciting ways to meet the challenges that a new millennium threw at them. Many schools have used the opportunities offered by this collaboration to tackle some of the deep-seated issues that have stifled the prospects of a generation of young people. There can be few more vivid examples of the changes taking place at a local level than the work of the Dearne Valley Education Partnership—a consortium of schools serving some of Yorkshire's most deprived wards, set amid a landscape of coal heaps that nature is slowly reclaiming. Though the preceding chapters have dealt with the achievements of individual schools, I was also keen to document what a group of schools has done to tackle profound social and economic challenges through an innovative approach to education. I was especially eager to explore the extent to which the work of consortia such as the Dearne Valley Education Partnership could herald a new era when such close cooperation between schools is the norm. As we shall see, the progress made by the partnership also casts light on the importance of a visionary project manager working across the schools, and the story of the Dearne Valley Education Partnership is told through the testimony of just such a person—Julianne Duffy.

It was a warm May day that allowed me to have lunch with Julianne al fresco, from an impressive vantage point overlooking a panorama of the Dearne Valley. We had met at the appropriately named Gannets Café—part of a new flagship nature reserve that is attracting wildlife enthusiasts from across the north of England. Making a beeline for the elevated veranda of this popular local eating place allowed us to enjoy a 180 degree sweep of this unlikely magnet for nature, known locally as Old Moor.

Carefully sculpted lakes and pools were dotted with water birds, their reed-fringed margins twitching with newly arrived warblers from Africa. Hillsides festooned with blossoming hawthorns and wild flowers added to the tapestry of colour. As we tucked into our food a soundtrack of chirruping tree sparrows from Yorkshire's largest colony rose above the clinking of crockery in the busy kitchen. As Julianne began to reveal the story of Old Moor and its hinterland, the profound changes that this landscape has witnessed in turn began to reveal themselves.

A landscape of change

A few decades ago this part of the Dearne Valley was a hive of mining activity—machinery, noise, grime, sweat, danger—populated by men whose life expectancy was lowered significantly through their day to day toil. What appear today as lush hillsides were once gigantic spoil heaps that have brought new contours to what was essentially a wide river valley. The industry that sustained this part of Yorkshire for so long is no more, and gone with it are the livelihoods of thousands of men whose skills and efforts are all but forgotten in a country where the soft hands of commuters bear witness to the prevailing service industries. There are families now living in the Dearne Valley that have not known employment in three generations.

It was Barnsley Council that first realised the potential of the site to welcome bearers of different tools—the beaks and webbed feet of water birds that were to make their home in the oasis that was created as man helped nature to reclaim Old Moor. But as well as ploughing funds into the creation of new habitat—augmenting what had already been created as mining subsidence formed wetlands such as Wath Ings—the council saw the potential for Old Moor as a place for *people* too. By creating a visitor centre and education room in former farm buildings, by designing an inspirational playground and by installing birdwatching hides overlooking the water, the council—in partnership with the Environment Agency—created a much-needed natural breathing space in the Dearne Valley. Such was the success and further potential of the reserve that the Royal Society for the Protection of Birds—Europe's largest environmental organisation—jumped at the opportunity to make this one of their most prominent wildlife sites in northern England, which now welcomes over 50,000 visitors a year. It is against this backdrop of change, and the huge social and economic problems that have sprung up from it, that we must set the story of regeneration in the Dearne Valley and the role that education is playing.

Waterbirds find sanctuary at Old Moor, where huge machines once extracted coal to power the industrial furnace of Britain

A spirit of collaboration

The children of the Dearne Valley Education Partnership reside in the triangle created by the settlements of Barnsley, Doncaster and Rotherham, and attend one of nine secondary schools or two special schools shared by the three local authorities, or the further education college. When Julianne took on the role of project manager for the partnership in 2002, education collaboration in the area was already well established. Major funding from Europe and elsewhere had allowed the three local authorities serving the region to set up a range of projects that aimed to tackle underachievement and improve the employment prospects for young people locally. With a background in social services and youth work—coupled with an entrepreneurial spirit and a 'can do' attitude—Julianne was ideally placed to take on the challenge of securing benefits for eleven schools with similar and different needs.

The Dearne Valley (marked with a dot •) in South Yorkshire

The Dearne Valley Education Partnership

Barnsley

The Foulstone School

The Dearne High School (Specialist Humanities College)
Wombwell High School (Specialist Humanities College)

Doncaster

Athelstane School (Special)
Northcliffe School
Mexborough School (Specialist Science College)

Rotherham

Swinton Community School (Specialist Maths and Computing College)
Wath Comprehensive School (Specialist Language College)
Rawmarsh Community School (Specialist Sports College)
St Pius X Catholic High School (Specialist Humanities College)
Milton School (Special)
Dearne Valley College (FE College)

Recent educational milestones in the Dearne Valley

July 1991 – Dearne Valley Partnership established

The partnership implemented a ten year plan to redevelop the area following the closure of local collieries during the 1980s. The partnership encompassed three local authorities —Barnsley, Doncaster and Rotherham—and received more than £150 million towards social and economic regeneration, which included promoting and developing education facilities in the area. Throughout this period the headteachers of six secondary and two special schools in the area worked together and shared good practice, to ensure that the disadvantaged communities received the support they needed. At this time, the school partnership was known as the Dearne Valley Secondary Heads Group.

March 2002 – Project manager joins team

A project manager (Julianne Duffy) was appointed, initially on a temporary contract to manage a substantial New Opportunities Fund Out of School Hours Learning grant and develop joint funding bids and partnership work. A ninth secondary school also joined the partnership.

January 2003 – College joins the partnership

Dearne Valley College joins the partnership and the project manager is appointed to manage a three year programme being funded through Rotherham Council called DeVeLOP— the Dearne Valley Learning Opportunities Partnership. The funding was granted to focus specifically on the Dearne Valley, following the benefits seen from the extensive work which had already been undertaken, and to build upon the established track record of educational partnership work.

March 2003 – Dearne Valley Partnership ceased operating

By 2003 it was felt that the original partnership had fulfilled its role and the regeneration work became spread more widely throughout South Yorkshire. However, collaborative working continued as the DeVeLOP project manager remained in post and the headteachers of the schools involved continued to meet on a regular basis. This resulted in a number of successful bids for specific projects across the schools, such as a major expansion of out of school hours learning, grants for teaching assistants and several arts projects.

April 2004 – Dearne Valley Education Partnership born

Two further secondary schools joined the partnership and the name was changed to reflect the fact that the partners now included eleven secondary schools and a college (which joined in 2003). Success locally led to additional funding for a two year pilot programme to appoint a transition advisor for all the partners, focusing on the transition for young people from Key Stage 4 to securing a positive destination for them, whether this is continuing in education, an apprenticeship or work with or without training. This was a bold and forward-looking move, as the area is not limited by local authority boundaries, which are in turn not recognised by learners.

September 2005 – Limited company status for the partnership

The Dearne Valley Education Partnership Ltd became a company limited by guarantee, providing continued opportunity to use the strength of the partnership to access joint funding and obtain other benefits of working together. The chair and vice-chair of the group are headteachers from the constituent schools, with the project manager of the partnership serving as the company secretary.

Present day – Continued investment in success

The Dearne Valley continues to be an area that requires a special focus, as Learning and Skills Council statistics show that achievement is significantly lower than that of surrounding boroughs. Positive feedback is being gained from external bodies for the work taking place—for example, from the Department for Education and Skills (DfES) who applauded the commitment to partnership working and the establishment of 'learning alliances'. Other partnerships have been formed in the region to widen the successes achieved in the Dearne Valley and attract other partners. It's clear, however, that further work is needed to raise aspiration, expectation and achievement in the Dearne Valley. This is further evidenced by the recent structural changes which have taken place in sub-regional partnerships and the recognition of the Sheffield City Region. Within the development plan for the region, the Dearne Valley is recognised as an area which continues to require special consideration.

'There is now a need to build on the achievements in the Dearne Valley and develop its role in a way that complements the focus on economic growth in the main urban centres. It has been agreed by the South Yorkshire local authorities to develop a new vision for the Dearne Valley.'

Monday	Tuesday
Meeting at Cadeby Henge with project archaeologist.*	DVEP Enterprise Co-ordinators' meeting.
Meeting with the new headteacher of Dearne High School to introduce him to the partnership and our aims/ways of working.	Meeting with DVC enterprise coordinator.
	Meeting at Foulstone School with head of MFL, organised for Business Enterpise South Yorkshire regarding engaging businesses who use languages.
Evening 'Quids In' meeting with young people from Believe Performing Arts Company regarding funding application—at Young People's Centre in Rotherham.	Meeting at Foulstone School regarding Comenius project monitoring and evaluation.

* Partnership bid with Society of the Don and Dearne, received £30,000 from Heritage Lottery Fund

The work of the partnership over the last five years has centred on the establishment of a series of discrete projects—usually funded from outside school budgets—that have addressed head on some of the key priorities for the schools. This manifests itself on a day to day basis by the schools taking advantage of Julianne's skills in a variety of ways, as can be seen from the detail of a typical working week.

Wednesday	Thursday	Friday
Attend Athelstane Special School to write Awards for All bid for Duke of Edinburgh rock climbing course and expedition equipment.	Meeting with assistant head-teacher of Swinton Community School regarding funding opportunities and looking at the International Schools Award.	DVEP Board Meeting with headteachers/principals of all DVEP partners.
Meeting with the opening learning centre manager and young people from Believe Performing Arts Company at Rawmarsh Community School.	Meeting with community links coordinator from St Pius X Catholic High School.	Meeting with head of construction at DVC regarding Cadeby Henge and opportunities for student involvement.
	14–19 Learning Strategy Meeting in Rotherham.	

A typical working week for Julianne Duffy

Innovating for education

An excellent example of collaborative working comes in the form of a European-scale staff development project organised with the financial support of the EU, as part of the Comenius programme. The aim of this three year project was to develop resources that could be used by teachers in four countries—Britain, Belgium, Greece and Spain. Teachers from one school in the partnership (Foulstone) met with colleagues from other European schools in order to develop the resources. When in the UK, European teachers visited local sites of heritage and artistic interest, such as the National Mining Museum and Yorkshire Sculpture Park. There were also smaller scale opportunities for students from the respective schools to get involved. Four students participated in the visits to European schools and further students were also partnered up and kept in touch via email, leading to greater awareness of other European cultures. The communication links also helped students and staff to improve their language skills. Outcomes from the project included a DVD and leaflet on wine making and another teaching resource linked to producing cotton—these resources focused on the industries in the area which have developed following the decline in their former traditional industries. The Comenius work carried out so far has been successful for the teachers taking part, but more schemes are being developed that will reach a wider group of students. Additional work is also being arranged that will allow teachers to cascade what they've learnt within their institution to the benefit of teachers and students.

> 'The Dearne Valley Education Partnership exists to further educational opportunities in the area—one of the most disadvantaged areas in England.' Julianne Duffy

Julianne believes that enterprise is a powerful force that can create change for young people in the Dearne Valley. And such was the extent of work needed to regenerate the region, the Dearne Valley once formed part of the largest Enterprise Zone in Europe.

Prior to enterprise education becoming a statutory entitlement in schools in 2005, the partnership successfully submitted a bid to the DfES and received a substantial Pathfinder grant which enabled staff from all subject areas to undertake training in curriculum enterprise development and host whole year Key Stage 3 activities. Sustainability came from the resources and lesson plans which were developed during the training and have been disseminated via the South Yorkshire e-sy info website. More recently, a new funding bid has resulted in a large grant for implementing enterprise at Key Stage 3. To help embed appropriate practice into schools Julianne runs a local Enterprise Group, comprising enterprise coordinators from all schools in the partnership who, appropriately, also meet at Old Moor—itself now becoming something of a hub for enterprise locally.

Other colleagues are pioneering different approaches to enhancing education in the Dearne Valley. Various opportunities exist to share good practice and develop new initiatives, including an advanced teaching and learning group coordinated by one of the schools in the partnership that works to introduce innovative teaching and learning approaches into the classroom. Curriculum leaders from across the Dearne Valley meet regularly to share practice and develop a common timetable which has led to cross boundary courses in a number of vocational areas, enhancing the opportunities for young people. Other examples are shared INSET days and invitations to training taking place across the partnership. Following on from presentations to the board of directors, there have been many occasions where other staff have visited partner institutions to share resources and good practice.

An inspirational local example of how students can provide the creative force for change in schools comes from the Believe Performing Arts Company, a group formed by year 8 and 9 students from Rawmarsh Community School. Not content just to run their own after school drama club, the group have instead set up a high profile theatre company, with the vision that it will be self-sustaining as soon as possible. Formal roles have been assigned, ranging from dance captain to musical director, all of which are held by students. Funding is being sought for a range of projects, including productions staged in a local theatre. The group made an application to a Rotherham-based funding body that embraces the spirit of the student voice by making a panel of young people entirely responsible for allocating funding. The students from the company had to answer a range of questions from the scrutinising panel of young people, while the adults sat outside the room! They were grilled on a range of issues to do with their project, including how inclusive it was and the degree to which it addressed issues in the Every Child Matters agenda. A letter confirming they had been awarded £5,000 for their project has just been received. The work of the Believe Performing Arts Company has benefited greatly from the support of Rawmarsh Community School's extended school coordinator. His work has also involved the setting up of a range of exciting clubs for students, including golf, environment, archaeology and horticulture groups.

Julianne Duffy (foreground) with members of the Believe Performing Arts Company

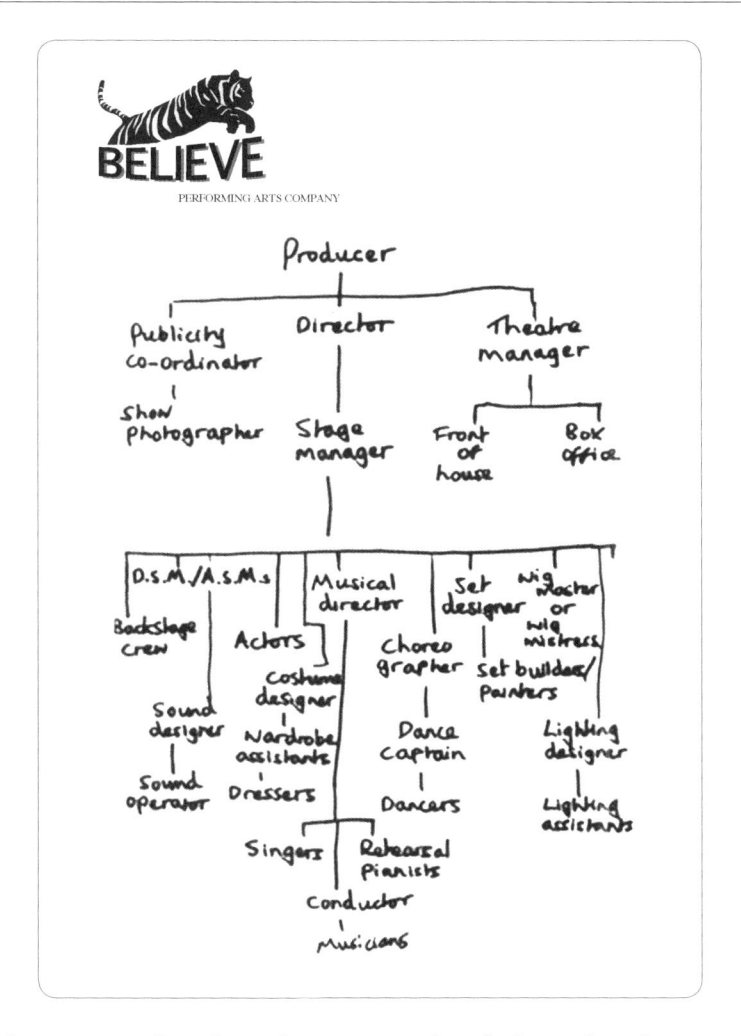

Students created a formal structure for their performing arts company

Further examples of student empowerment are easily found within the partnership. In another school, students formed ABC (Anti Bullying Club), an action group which aimed to stamp out bullying. Through a poster campaign, meetings and a range of other work, these students are helping to make bullying socially unacceptable. This is all the more impressive given that some of the students in the action group had suffered from some unpleasant bullying themselves. This is linking to a 'Beat Bullying' campaign in the college. Transition work is focusing on ensuring that bullying at school is not carried through to the next destination. Peer activists, again students who have experienced bullying, are supporting other students in various ways.

On another front, the schools within the partnership have also been addressing the workforce remodelling agenda in order to ensure that teachers are freed up to teach. As part of this development a workforce remodelling audit was carried out which sought to establish the extent to which schools had managed to embrace this important initiative. A key outcome of this work was the appointment of cover supervisors across the partnership to alleviate the administrative burden on teachers. The benefits and strengths of collaboration were most evident here as one school—which had developed job descriptions, person specifications, adverts and interview criteria—shared this with all other partners, resulting in a consistent recruitment approach and parity of salaries. Much time was saved in developing the recruitment strategy and this sharing also helped partners to avoid issues with retention, which can be problematic and time consuming.

Advantages have been gained through the constituted nature of the partnership. It was established as a company limited by guarantee in September 2005, which has brought with it a number of benefits. It allowed the partnership to be recognised as a group in its own right, as well as allowing it to apply for additional funding sources, cement links with other partners and generally provide a practical demonstration of the progress of the partnership. Headteachers within the partnership have applauded the efforts of Julianne and clearly recognise that much has been achieved through innovative collaborative working. One headteacher commented that out of all the external meetings and all the external groups he is part of in the Dearne Valley (there are many!), this partnership is the only one he does not have to attend but *always* does. When time is so short, this speaks volumes.

One headteacher has gone on record to state that of all the external groups he has been part of in the Dearne Valley (there have been many!), the latest partnership is the one he is most happy to be part of.

The need for sustainability

When asked how she judges the success of her work, Julianne is absolutely clear that the *sustainability* of the programmes she facilitates is her key criterion. Though originally working towards specific funding targets, she is now more focused on high quality outcomes for young people and their community. Nevertheless, as funding is now running out for projects that were begun thanks to successful grant applications, accessing new funds for projects is still an important part of Julianne's job.

The formal constituted nature of the partnership has done much to secure its position locally and regionally, and has helped to attract major education funding to the Dearne Valley. If its success is to be maintained into the future, then Julianne believes the partnership needs to continue to occupy its high profile position, taking advantage of new forms of constitution as the opportunity arises. With the government eager to support much more formal collaboration between schools—with scenarios as radical as sharing a governing body on the table—the schools within the partnership will want to investigate which model will give them the greatest chance of thriving in the uncertain world of tomorrow.

The pioneering work of the Dearne Valley Education Partnership has attracted considerable interest from other parts of the UK, with Julianne invited to speak to colleagues wrestling with similar challenges in places such as the London borough of Ealing. Here, the challenge is how schools in one authority can join together, in a genuine way, in a spirit of partnership.

Dearne Valley headlines

- ACCOUNTANT LAUNCHES STRATEGY TO IMPROVE REGION'S PROSPERITY
- DEARNE VALLEY PARTNERSHIP EXCEEDING EXPECTATIONS
- HOPE OF 2,000 NEW JOBS AS SERVICE CENTRE IS COMPLETED
- PACKAGE OF INVESTMENT PAYS OFF
- FORMER PIT SITE SETTING FOR LEISURE DEVELOPMENT
- COMMERCIAL BASES ARE RISING FROM INDUSTRIAL WASTELANDS
- PUPILS DIG IN TO FIND A FRESH-AIR WAY OF LEARNING
- DEARNE STAGES TOP CONFERENCE

Julianne is happy to admit that the partnership can do more to widen the scope of its work and deepen its impact—and this begins with marketing itself better so that local service providers can understand better how they can become involved. She also feels that even more could be done by pooling the resources of the three boroughs represented in the partnership; this may become possible with the Sheffield City Region and South Yorkshire boroughs continuing to recognise the Dearne Valley. This would provide a cost-effective way of ensuring that the Dearne communities benefit from *both* the local borough provision and the opportunities from neighbouring areas to extend choice and enhance achievement.

The nature of 14–19 education continues to change and develop with specialised diplomas coming online in 2008. The partnership is seizing the initiative by submitting an application to develop and deliver joint Dearne Valley diplomas. This will continue to embed the collaboration between the schools and college and hopefully benefit the students as much as possible. Capacity is always an issue when extending and enhancing provision and the partnership is tentatively looking to create a Dearne Valley 14–19 Centre of Excellence utilising a building which has recently become available. Much work still needs to be done in this area but the vision to create such a facility is firmly upheld by the partnership.

The 'secrets' of success

What does the work of the Dearne Valley Education Partnership tell us about the role of collaboration in school improvement and classroom change? And building on that, what factors led to the success of the work undertaken? There appear to be at least six interrelated factors.

The power of genuine collaboration

The success of the partnership shows clearly that by working together schools can be a much more effective force for change in communities where there are deep-seated social and economic challenges. The schools in the partnership are managing to emerge from these economic and social pressures, and through their innovative practice providing examples of work which has been nationally recognised. In order to take advantage of these benefits, however, it required a bold move on the part of the participating schools to invest time and resources in making the partnership work. A formal constitution has also clearly helped the partnership schools to lever in funding and generally be taken more seriously by other strategic bodies working in the region. A key part of being in such a partnership is the need to keep up to date with new and emerging forms of collaboration, in order to bring maximum benefits to the participating schools. This has been recognised by the Dearne Valley Education Partnership through, for example, their adoption of limited company status, which is bringing new benefits. The commitment to genuine collaborative working stands out as the most significant factor in the success of the partnership.

Money can help

While some of the examples in this book illustrate success in schools that have not relied heavily on additional funding, the Dearne Valley Education Partnership has clearly taken great strides forward thanks to the funding committed by the schools to Julianne's post as coordinator. This can very much be seen as an investment, however, since Julianne has been able to bring in more than £250,000 in additional funding for the schools over the last three years for a range of new projects. This cash injection has made a very real difference to the scope of the work undertaken in the partnership schools. Quite simply, several high profile projects now taking place would not have happened without it.

Innovative approaches

Creative approaches have certainly been a hallmark of the work of the Dearne Valley Education Partnership. Thanks especially to Julianne's imaginative spirit, many unusual and inspiring initiatives and projects have been carried out that have used fresh approaches to tackle deep-seated problems. Two examples are the distinctive approach to enterprise infused into a range of school projects, and the advanced teaching and learning group which Julianne supports in schools. It is worth noting here that the depth of the challenge facing the partnership schools *required* that creative solutions were found; the status quo was unimaginable.

A focus on sustainability

The partnership continues to concentrate on how it can build on past success to ensure continuity for the participating schools. While this attitude has enabled it to take advantage of new opportunities in the past, it also means it is constantly looking to the future. Julianne sees this sustainability as the key factor on which the future success of the partnership should be judged. It requires that careful planning is carried out so that lulls in action do not result in lost opportunities.

Student empowerment

Several examples of recent projects show that the partnership is committed to enabling students to reach their potential, often in surprising ways. The Believe Performing Arts Company provides just one example of how, by handing over responsibility to young people, impressive educational outcomes are possible. The partnership is helping to show that, although education is often undervalued among parents in these disadvantaged parts of Yorkshire, students are capable of very high quality work.

Getting the right person to lead the partnership

Any group of schools considering working in a formal partnership obviously needs to give very careful consideration to the person they appoint to carry out the role of coordinator. The 'can do' attitude of Julianne has clearly made a big difference to the success of the Dearne Valley Education Partnership. Her ability to use her initiative, work without close supervision and provide a model for effective networking has brought significant benefits to the partnership schools. Partnership working does, therefore, require an especially effective overall 'driver' to provide leadership for the participating schools, which often have slightly different needs. The ability of schools to find such as leader has a major effect on the quality of outcomes for all.

How transferable is this work?

The effective collaborative work of the Dearne Valley Education Partnership would not have been possible without the belief and cooperation of the schools themselves—schools that, given the challenges that confront them every day, could for forgiven for turning inwards rather than outwards in their quest for solutions. Although there's clearly a long way still to go to before the area emerges fully from its current challenges, the many breakthroughs achieved by the partnership to date demonstrate that there is much hope—and an expectation that, together, a brighter future will be created. The fact that the schools in the partnership are united by a core vision for the kind of future they want to create helps them to move towards this vision in a spirit of teamwork and collaboration. Schools wishing to mirror the success of the partnership should take heart from this, while readying themselves for similar levels of engagement. They too can reap widespread benefits.

The other success factors identified are clearly key principles to be borne in mind by schools considering similar partnership arrangements. Most are perfectly replicable elsewhere, though the specific focus of other partnerships may require a different emphasis. Any partnership is, however, only effective if it has an energetic leader to move things forward, to support and encourage, and to help individual schools to look beyond their horizons and try new approaches. It is significant that in Julianne Duffy the partnership schools have found such a leader, who has gone beyond her initial focus on fundraising to set her sights on much grander goals; goals that are making a difference to the lives of the young people of the Dearne Valley. As more and more schools consider the benefits of collaborative working—and begin to realise that formal constituted approaches can reap far reaching benefits—they would be wise also to remind themselves that to achieve their dreams they need to place considerable emphasis on bringing in the right person to spearhead their efforts.

The first six chapters have concentrated on changes taking place at the whole school level. In the following chapter, I want to delve deeper into individual schools by exploring work at the classroom and departmental level. Here, we shall see that change is taking place even though in some cases the school is not achieving wider success.

Chapter 7

Stories from Successful Classrooms and Departments

> *'If you think you're too small to make a difference, then you've never shared a bed with a mosquito.'* Ken Dunn

Change in some schools is not taking place through whole school initiatives, such as those described in the earlier chapters of this book; instead, it is taking place at the classroom or departmental level. While it is true that no whole school change is possible without a parallel change at these finer levels, there are some striking examples of work taking place at the classroom or departmental level that has not yet resulted in major institutional change. In other schools, it is the combined effect of work taking place at these finer levels that is resulting in the specific successes of individual schools. I want to use this closing chapter of case studies, therefore, to focus in more detail on success in such classrooms and departments.

It strikes me that there are several good reasons for including the stories of individual teachers in the book. First, I wish to acknowledge that success at the classroom or departmental level is possible even if the school is not widely recognised as successful. There is an empowering message here for those teachers and departmental leaders who are creating a powerful impact, but whose work is, by necessity, limited to a portion of students in any one institution. Second, by recognising that much can be achieved at the classroom or departmental level—irrespective of the other constraints facing the school—it gives hope to those who feel that there is a lot still to do to create the kind of school which they would be proud of.

Some of the schools featured in this chapter *are* achieving wider success, built on work at classroom and departmental level. These are included to provide examples of the kind of work at this finer scale that can result in more profound institutional benefits. The chapter also gives the opportunity for individual teachers and departmental leaders to place on record their particular triumphs more specifically, in a manner that has not been possible in the preceding chapters of the book.

This chapter has been assembled based on visits and interviews with a wide range of teachers and departmental leaders in a variety of schools around the country. Some, for obvious reasons, have chosen to remain anonymous here. I begin first with stories at the classroom level and move on to consider departmental success, before making some concluding remarks about what has been said.

Transforming PE

The work of Thomas Doyle (a pseudonym) shows us that remarkable results can be achieved even in a short space of time and with minimal support from other members of your department. Thomas joined his school (a comprehensive in England) in September 2006 to teach PE in a department that he soon realised was simply not providing an acceptable level of education to its students. Low expectations, lack of planning and poor teacher morale had resulted in PE taking a back seat at the school when it should have been a major force. The head of department—recruited internally after the previous post-holder had left the school—had clearly failed to switch students on to PE, and it was seen by many as an excuse to take things easy, even at GCSE level.

In 2006, GCSE success was dismal, with only twenty-seven per cent of students achieving A*–C in a school which on other measures performed higher than the national average. Thomas knew that his experience of delivering high quality PE lessons in his previous school could be used to galvanise interest in the subject in this new setting. In September that same year he set to work immediately with his new year 11 students to drive up expectations and provide learning experiences that genuinely engaged students. The barriers initially seemed huge, with student behaviour and attitudes being very poor and departmental standards lamentable. He realised that it was going to be a long haul to bring round students—and exam fortunes. Thomas's enthusiasm was curbed further when he realised that his GCSE group had only covered half of the expected syllabus in year 10, leaving him with a huge chunk to get through in the two terms that remained before the exams were upon the students.

Through an unswerving commitment and a tremendous amount of hard work, the fruits of Thomas's work became clear when the GCSE results were revealed in August 2007—the A*–C pass rate had jumped to fifty per cent, a spectacular rise considering the challenges Thomas faced. In addition to a positive student response to a range of exciting new lessons, Thomas believes that these impressive results are in no small part due to twenty out of thirty-three students turning up to special after school revision classes he staged after Easter. What is even more remarkable however—and he would probably be rewarded with a knighthood if the results had reflected the whole-school work of a headteacher—is that ninety-six per cent of his current year 11 students are predicted to gain A*–C grades in PE. This is simply incredible given the department's performance only two years earlier!

I interviewed Thomas at the end of his summer holiday, a time when teachers are usually well justified in switching off from school to recharge their batteries. While he had made a point of taking time out to holiday with his family, Thomas had also been busy marking, and I was intrigued to know more. It turned out that he had been carrying out postal correspondence with students in order to mark drafts of their GCSE coursework, itself worth ten per cent of the overall mark. It soon became clear that this dedication to the role and a willingness to go that extra mile permeates everything Thomas does for his school. The results are equally evident in the high uptake of sports clubs he runs at lunchtime and after school—again a significant achievement in a school where extra-curricular sport has been allowed to wallow.

Lunchtime sport clubs

Shown below are the sports clubs run by Thomas (asterisked*). Note that Thomas is only in school Monday, Tuesday Wednesday so that is why he doesn't do clubs on the other two days. Lunchtime is from 12.30 to 1.30 p.m. and clubs run for half an hour so that he can do two per lunchtime. Most of the swimming is unstaffed as the lifeguards at the pool are present.

As well as lunchtime clubs there are a number of after school activities. Thomas runs run a Young Leaders' Award on a Thursday from 3.45 to 5.00 p.m.

	12.30 – 1.00 p.m.	1.00 – 1.30 p.m.
Monday	Yr 8 Football Yr 7, 8, 9 Badminton*	Yr 10, 11 Badminton*
Tuesday	Yr 11 Swimming All years Squash Swimming*	Yr 9, 10, 11 Basketball*
Wednesday	Yr 9 Football Yr 7, 8 Basketball* Yr 7, 8 Swimming	Yr 7 Rugby All years Dance*
Thursday	All Years Indoor Hockey (split pitch) Yr 9 Swimming	
Friday	Yr 7 Football Yr 10 Swimming	Yr 10 Football

Chapter 7: Stories from Successful Classrooms and Departments | 185

How can a teacher, I pondered, manage to transform learning in such a short space of time, without the support of this fellow departmental colleagues? What are the secrets of Thomas's approach to teaching that single him out as one of the rising stars of PE teaching in this country? In short, it turned out, two simple factors—the highest of expectations, coupled with the desire to plan and deliver creative lessons that really get children thinking.

Thomas spoke passionately about a number of recent lessons he had taught, all of which showed these factors in abundance (see box below). His passion for his subject shone through, and clearly shines through to his students too. One day, near to the end of last term, a student in his class watched him speak about the lesson to come and then quietly turned to him and said, 'You love PE don't you, Mr Doyle?' Thanks in part to this boundless enthusiasm, many of his students now clearly *love* PE too, with several considering careers in a subject that was previously considered 'a bit of a doss' at the school.

Assessing health and safety hazards in PE

This lesson was designed to provide an engaging way for students to learn about the health and safety hazards associated with a school gym. It was taught as part of a unit on ways to minimise the risk of injury in sport.

It began, somewhat mysteriously, by the students finding the door to the gym locked. On asking why, they were told that the gym had been left in a terrible state by a previous group (in fact it had been set up that way by Thomas prior to the start of the lesson!). In pairs, students were issued with a recording sheet and clipboard, and were told to go and find seventeen health and safety hazards present in the gym. These ranged from water spilt on the floor to the balance beam not being pegged in place.

After ten minutes or so the group came together to discuss what they had found and what the implications would be for people using the room, together with how the hazards could be put right. During the discussion several students noticed hazards that had *not* been set up by Thomas—unexpected and needing attention in their own right! The lesson ended with students actually making the room safe. Homework was to write up a report on the risks that had been found and how they could be minimised.

Thomas felt that it was the elements of mystery and discovery in the lesson that ensured it was a real success with students, and it remains a popular favourite with GCSE classes at this school. Significantly, this lesson's creative elements are quite unlike any of the lessons that were taught in the PE department prior to Thomas taking up his post.

Chapter 7: Stories from Successful Classrooms and Departments

1. Square w/bars not fixed in.
2. Condemned mat to stand on.
3. Broken hoop on floor.
4. Buck with wonky legs.
5. No crash mat to land on.
6. Bench against wall with no hooks in bar.
7. Brake not on vault.
8. Bench in front of door.
9. Water on floor.
10. Beam not pegged in place.
11. Jumper on floor.
12. No mats under ropes.
13. Window hook leaning against wall.
14. Ropes not out fully.
15. Mat trolley half out.
16. Mud on floor.
17. Litter on floor.
18. No safety grids on windows.

> **Health and Safety in Physcial Education**
>
> The school gym has been set up for a year 10 apparatus lesson. Unfortunately the teacher was rushed and has not set the equipment up in a safe way. Walk round the gym and see if you can identify the 17 safety hazards.
>
> 1. _____
> 2. _____
> 3. _____
> 4. _____
> 5. _____
> 6. _____
> 7. _____
> 8. _____
> 9. _____
> 10. _____
> 11. _____
> 12. _____
> 13. _____
> 14. _____
> 15. _____
> 16. _____
> 17. _____

I was eager to find out more about what is was like for a teacher to effectively provide leadership in a department when the subject leader was not up to scratch. It struck me that this would certainly have caused me *considerable* anguish had I been in the same situation—not least because it brings into question the professionalism of colleagues. While Thomas admitted it had been a considerable challenge, he also felt it was his duty to get the best for the students, even if that meant taking control by suggesting he taught all the GCSE students himself! The head of department's willingness to allow Thomas to do this speaks volumes about how out of touch his own leadership had become. Yet the benefits for students are clear and this is what matters to Thomas.

Other people have begun to notice the inspirational work of Thomas. The headteacher, other leaders and the governors have all commented on his outstanding first year at the school. Students are now respected in the department and in turn give more respect back to their teachers. Some now talk of PE being their favourite subject. More parents are attending review evenings and many positive comments are being made about students' passion for PE.

One of the most empowering messages that I draw out from Thomas's work is that it shows us that even in very challenging circumstances in a department, powerful changes are possible. While these changes would not be happening without Thomas's dedication, expertise and professionalism, they show us that profound classroom change *can* happen—and is happening—if we want it badly enough.

As Thomas spoke about his achievements it became clear that he is very proud of his successes during his first year at the school. Although not new to success in a teaching role, Thomas had not previously witnessed the dramatic transformation that has occurred since he took up this new post. He has taken considerable satisfaction from the results and changing attitudes of his students, and rightly so. But he has also emerged with something more tangible: a real confidence in his abilities as a teacher that will allow him to push on towards even greater achievements. I'm sure we've not heard the last of the career highlights of this impressive young PE teacher.

Exciting ICT

Jan Blair, ICT teacher at St Sampson's Secondary School in Guernsey, is another example of a teacher who has enriched lessons in a variety of creative ways. Beginning in year 7, she decided to liven up the system life cycle by getting the students to make Christmas decorations on this theme, converting a drab ICT suite into an eye-catching space adorned with tinsel mobiles! The result was a learning resource that got round the 'rule' that no Christmas decorations are allowed in ICT rooms, and the project excited students so much that some parents even got involved in making decorations. A further development in year 7 was the use of role play in project work, with students making hats and badges to signify their role (manager, designer, researcher, and so on). A key part of this work involved students using team building skills in order to achieve a high quality outcome, including negotiation and delegation. The use of hands-on teaching and learning strategies has proved especially beneficial for these younger children.

The culmination of Jan's efforts has seen GCSE students in year 10 and 11 carrying out real tasks for real businesses. Examples include two students who have designed the new school website, another student who based his project on the local marina and another duo promoting a Scout group. Other examples show students taking a greater degree of ownership in key areas of the school, all as part of their ICT course. A year 10 student who did all the lighting for school productions, taking the lead with this highly technical aspect of performing arts at the school, used these skills for his GCSE project. As well as creating a lot of enthusiasm, this work has enabled students to gain valuable skills for the real world—and they end up with a successful project which they can make reference to in their curricula vitae. There's also been a positive response from local businesses, helping to enhance the school's profile in the community. One example that is creating wider benefit is the link with Specsavers' head office, which has resulted in students being provided with knowledge, support and practical help with some specific projects.

Brain-based learning

Sarah Todd is an Advanced Skills Teacher at Stanchester Community School in Somerset who has used training in so-called 'brain-based' learning in order to improve her lessons. The main catalyst for this work was her attendance at an inspirational programme organised by the University of the First Age (UFA), a charity working to promote more innovative teaching informed by research into the brain and learning. After becoming a UFA 'fellow' and being exposed to a raft of stimulating new approaches, Sarah immediately set to work to embed fresh approaches into her lessons. The need to inspire students with different learning preferences was the first area she tackled, together with a drive to ensure that student feedback was used to judge the success of learning strategies and also the quality of teaching itself.

Keen to spread the successes she had observed in her own classroom, Sarah set up workshops which were made available to teaching staff on an optional basis—with over fifty per cent of colleagues turning up. Many teachers were similarly excited by the new approaches, and slowly a culture of sharing good practice more widely began. This work led on to whole school 'Super Learning Days' for students and 'Learning to Learn' events for parents, which managed to support a culture for learning in departments and help parents to understand their role in their children's learning. It is significant that during these events everyone was seen to be learning—and that included staff too. This provided the impetus for additional staff to make progress in their own classrooms, some of whom simply needed the confidence to try out approaches that, though unconventional, they felt would be appropriate for their learners.

Sarah also made progress at the classroom level through an innovative team teaching project which has continued for four years. This has sought to use collaboration between teachers in the geography department to encourage more risk taking in the classroom to develop learning. As a result, students regularly sing and dance, make models out of scrap paper and/or play dough, and use games and an interactive whiteboard to enhance learning. Students have commented on how they like having the two teaching styles that team teaching can bring with it. This also helped to take Sarah out of her comfort zone to try unusual approaches which have brought a wide range of benefits—not least for the examination results of the students who have used the new approaches. Convinced of the value of such approaches, Sarah is now a firm advocate of team teaching, which she describes as a 'fantastic opportunity'. She is also clear, though, that it does need time to establish ground rules and jointly plan—sacrifices that have clearly been worth taking in this Somerset school.

The need for risk taking

Emily McNab (a pseudonym) provides an example of how risk taking in a single classroom can provide the catalyst for wider change in a department and school. Over a four year period Emily carried out a concerted effort to improve the educational experience for GCSE students at a comprehensive school in England. Working in a geography department, Emily identified the need to raise aspirations for year 10 and 11 students who, although performing at a satisfactory level, were in danger of complacency and underachievement. Though there were pockets of good practice taking place at the school, there was also much inertia, with some colleagues having taught at the school for over twenty years and delivering rather stale lessons to students. Furthermore, the most recent Ofsted inspection had been lukewarm in its praise of teaching approaches and there was clearly much that could be done to switch students on to learning. The school's GCSE results suggested that some students were coasting rather than being stretched.

The hallmark of Emily's work was imagination, coupled with the notion that calculated risk in the classroom took students—and teachers—beyond familiar shores towards new and exciting horizons for learning. Emily tried out a multitude of approaches over the course of her first couple of years in post, some working, others failing spectacularly, but mostly resulting in high levels of motivation from students. Vitally, Emily adopted a very reflective approach and regularly sought the views of other staff and students on what had worked and why. In the initial stages this feedback was gained mainly in opportunistic ways, as part of lessons or occasional observations by the head of department. Emily developed a personal mission statement to guide her efforts during this period: 'My students deserve better!'

Emily's innovative teaching and learning approaches in geography

The following approaches were attempted by Emily during her two years in post:

- Advanced role play with students getting involved in real life community issues (e.g. the building of wind turbines locally)
- Puppet shows, news programmes and radio broadcasts to explore the effects of natural hazards on people in different countries
- Real life geographical learning (e.g. writing magazine articles on topical themes, working with local businesses on human geography topics, researching and preparing a new map of the town)
- Extended enquiries over several weeks, allowing students to work at their own pace, structure their own learning and evaluate their work
- Making international links using the internet to find and make contact with named people who were affected by incidents relating to geography in the news, rather than relying on an out of date textbook
- Entering competitions to inspire students and raise expectations, resulting in several winners from her classes

Though some of Emily's colleagues were sceptical that the techniques would be successful in this somewhat traditional school—including her own head of department—they began to be won round by positive feedback from students on their lessons with Emily. Teachers of other subjects started to notice that students were speaking positively about Miss McNab. The headteacher noticed that the average marks of students in Emily's GCSE classes were on an upward trend, and the impressive end of year test results gave added credence to her efforts to make learning more exciting.

Not resting on her laurels, Emily then began to take things further by strengthening her working relationship with students. She initiated a regular 'student review' session which turned on its head the conventional notion of how this takes place, with students providing *her* with feedback on how she could improve her teaching. This heralded something of a breakthrough for the school, which had not been used to such extensive student consultation on teaching and learning. Initially Emily had to fend off criticism from old timers who felt that students had very little constructive to offer in such consultations; they clearly felt rather threatened by the idea of students commenting openly on their teaching. The success of Emily's work in this area, however, soon resulted in students asking other teachers why *they* didn't give opportunities for their students to comment on their teaching, and a few bowed to the pressure and gave it a go too, with worthwhile results.

Though by no means fully embedded into the school, the geography department has embraced many of the approaches attempted by Emily. Some teachers beyond this department are starting to benefit too, as Emily has been asked to present to staff meetings some of the creative lessons that really got students talking. A small group of teachers are regularly benefiting from student feedback on their teaching and the possibility of a working group to consider wider school benefits of this approach has been suggested by the head. The impact of Emily's efforts have clearly been noticed at senior leadership level in her school, as she has been encouraged to consider a career as an Advanced Skills Teacher. Emily's advice to other teachers who want to make changes in a school is: 'Go for it!—nothing will change if students always get the same kind of lessons from the same kind of teachers. They deserve better!'

The needs of more able students

Peter Griffin (a pseudonym) has battled to promote the needs of more able students in his mathematics classroom, despite lack of support from his head of department and the school leadership team. Peter works in a school in the north of England that has recently emerged from Special Measures. It serves a very troubled catchment area, which has such high levels of unemployment that it is placed in the lowest band in the country based on socio-economic data. Despite many challenges the school does attract a number of very able students who, despite lack of parental support, are capable of high grades at GCSE. Sometimes, these students can be swallowed up by the wider pressures of running a challenging school, and are at risk of underachievement. However, in Peter's classroom he is making great strides forward to challenge and inspire these students so they can be enabled to reach their potential.

I visited Peter during a busy day prior to the start of study leave for year 11 students, and as soon as I entered his classroom it was clear that this was a teacher who commanded a great deal of respect from his students. I observed him work with a top set who were given a range of stimulating and thought-provoking mathematical problems, all aimed at getting students thinking for themselves and developing the capacity to come up with a range of solutions—without undue reliance on their teacher. While the degree of challenge was striking in Peter's classroom, it was the rapport that he had with his students that was most impressive. Through his language and his actions it was clear that this was a teacher who *respected* his students and wanted the very best from them. In turn, the students responded very positively, and at the end of the lesson I even heard one thanking him—not something I used to hear very often from students in the school in which I spent most of my teaching career.

Peter's success is made all the more remarkable when you realise that he is on something of a one-man mission to challenge and inspire more able students at his school. It is clear that most of the other staff have other agendas, and there seems to be a feeling that more able students will 'get along fine on their own'. Worryingly, even Peter's head of department has not taken their needs seriously.

It appears that the behavioural challenges facing many staff on a day to day basis have clouded their view of what differentiation should look like in the contemporary classroom. The leadership team too have not fully appreciated the efforts that Peter is making to raise aspirations, and even though he has taken the school's Maths Challenge team to a high placing in the regional final, his passion for challenging *all* students has not resulted in whole school measures that are benefiting a wider group of students. However, the fact that Peter is starting to get very impressive examination results, coupled with unusually high levels of motivation from often disaffected students, means that his leaders cannot for much longer ignore the success he is achieving and the changes he is making to the young people in his lessons. In his own way, Peter is saying 'I did it here!' and showing by example how others can do it too. Peter is making changes that can lead the school towards a much brighter future.

A focus on science

Tim Gamble and Karen Faulkner teach science at Northampton Academy, a school serving a socially diverse and economically deprived catchment area in a quiet corner of central England. Although the school is one of the government's flagship City Academies—and has received significant funding from an external sponsor (the United Learning Trust) as well as visits from Tony Blair and HRH The Princess Royal—it is a school that has had to wrestle with the challenges that come with driving up standards in an area where education has not traditionally been high on the list of priorities for a significant proportion of the population.

The new academy building, shaped engagingly like a fish, has been occupied since January 2006 and grew out of ageing premises where the academy was launched in 2004. Many of the staff currently working at the school, including Tim, previously taught at school's predecessor. The success of Tim (head of curriculum family—science and technology) and Karen (Key Stage 4 leader for the academy and head of biology) provides a stirring example of how work in an individual department can flourish, and how passionate teachers can help provide the lead for some significant whole school changes.

I visited the school on one of the few dry days in July, during a summer which may well become nicknamed the 'English monsoon', and the smart blue blazers of the students provided a welcome reminder that the sky above should be that colour in summer!

The examination results of the students in this part of Northamptonshire have not traditionally been inspiring, and a key challenge for departments at the school has been to give students the confidence to believe in themselves. The science department at Northampton Academy has been very proactive in this area, providing a practical example of how the school motto 'The best in everyone' can work on a daily basis in the classroom. An important part of this work has been the effort by Karen to *involve* students more systematically in lessons. One example is her 'thoughtboards' approach, which encourages students to record important facts or opinions about the lesson on sticky notes to be shared with others. These could be about the content of the lesson, how it made the students feel or the method of teaching and learning. The notes themselves are sometimes placed on a 'progress pillar' in Karen's classroom, which is used as a metaphor for how performance can be improved, written by Karen. On the day of my visit there were students' thoughts on a whole raft of topics on display, some with suggestions for how performance could be improved. The success of the thoughtboards has resulted in Karen being asked to write up the technique in a major education magazine for teachers.

I was invited by Karen to take a look inside her classroom where there were other examples of students' work to see. As soon as I entered, I could not fail to notice what a vibrant learning environment it was: X-rays of mysterious animals were pinned up on the walls, exotic plants grew up from colourful plant pots and striking posters and students' work greeted learners on arrival. In the corridor outside the classroom, displays of 'science in the news' and 'careers in science', put together and regularly updated by a teaching assistant, helped students to see that this is a *living* subject, with real relevance to their lives, not just another GCSE to take.

For his own part Tim, among other things, has breathed new life into the often dry topic of teacher feedback to students through a range of new approaches. One that stood out is the use of a written teacher comment on students' work to stimulate students' own written comments, which ranged from a direct response to the teacher's advice, to suggestions for how they are going to tackle a target set for them. This has helped students to look beyond the marks that are usually placed on their work and begin a genuine dialogue around how they can improve their performance, in the true spirit of assessment for learning. Another of Tim's ideas is the 'SciTech Bulletin' a weekly update for staff in the faculty which frequently contains advice on enriching lessons through practical examples from other classrooms. The particular example he showed me encouraged teachers to allow more student choice in lessons, with suggestions for how this might be done. Tim also handed me a CD to take away which his colleagues in the department had put together, part of a school-wide effort to document and share good practice. I spent some time later trawling through the inspiring documents on the CD, which I would have found very welcome at various stages of my own teaching career.

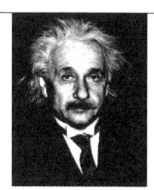

SciTech bulletin
Monday 1st October

Autumn is the season of mists and mellow fruitfulness
Welcome to week six !

1. Meetings : there is no Academy meeting this Monday, but KS4 Science teachers please remember we have a briefing from Sue after school about intervention strategies and group changes in Year 11. On Thursday we have our second intake evening. Many thanks to everyone who contributed to the first, and made it such a success – the displays were splendid and drew many compliments. Well done ! Please see Ron or Alison in good time so that they can organise who does what this week.
2. Registers : do please be diligent in submitting lesson registers promptly : we are still missing one or two almost every day, and we have to improve on that. Make it a priority please.
3. Performance management : the deadline for passing the completed documents to Peter is this Friday – the 12th. It's important that we stick to this. If you anticipate difficulties with this please let Peter and myself know straight away – don't just wait for it to be discovered ! In the same way for those Science staff involved in the lesson observation programme, remember that you need to complete the observations, and pass copies to me, by the end of this week. Many thanks !
4. Reports : our new reporting system runs for the first time from today until Friday 19th. Training sessions will be available from Anne Hill in how to use it. Please make an early start because the deadline is absolute – it cannot be extended. Programme leaders please monitor the process and keep us to schedule ! If a student is on your list but you have never seen them, leave their report blank. If you have seen them even once you should complete the report in full. If a group is shared between two teachers, (including sixth form groups), only one should complete the report. Programme leaders will advise which one.
5. Use of triage : we are trying as an academy to be very consistent in the use of the triage room : students should only be sent there by Sheila Porter, or the SMT member on call. As a class teacher or support teacher you simply pass the student, their work, and relevant information to the block supervisor. Don't try to send them yourself !
6. Science equipment requisitions : we've had a problem or two with late requests recently ! Teachers - please make every reasonable effort to submit your requisitions in good time; technicians - please make every reasonable effort to assist with any last minute problems that do arise!

Have an excellent week
Allgoodthings ...

   ..... Tim

Last week's famous face was of course Richard Dawkins – well done Sue !

You will have spotted by now that we are working through the alphabet, and this week is "E". No prizes for the name – too obvious !

Focus this week

"What level are you working at? .. and what is your target level ? ... and what do you need to do to improve?"

These are questions typically whispered to students by the inspector in your lesson. Of course the worst possible answers are "Dunno", "Don't care", and "Don't want to" ! Thankfully these are very rare, but it's not rare to find students who can't answer the questions, even when the information is written on a form in the front of their book ! Evidently they don't read or don't remember the forms, and this is not really surprising.

The only way to keep these ideas alive is to use and refer to them every day. Assessment is for learning, not just for exams.

As a start, next time you are explaining the learning objectives, why not explain what level or grade each one is set at. Next time you review what has been learned, why not explain what level or grade it is worth. Why not .... ?

"Perfection of means and confusion of goals seems to characterise our age"

   ...Albert Einstein

A weekly bulletin helps to galvanise interest in specific aspects of the work of Tim's faculty

Going beyond their subject specialisms, Tim and Karen have begun to provide whole school leadership for creative teaching and learning approaches. They were the creative force behind a Teaching and Learning Group that set itself the task of providing support for all subject areas in the quest to turn satisfactory into outstanding lessons. One outcome of this group was a 'Wonderwall', which was envisioned as a place to go to learn more about tried and tested teaching approaches across the school using record cards completed by different teachers. The long-term goal was to assemble this into a comprehensive practical handbook for staff, to serve as a continual point of reference when in need of inspiration. Though not all departments were able to sustain their involvement with this initiative, within science it remains an important way of sharing good practice and encouraging others to try out new approaches.

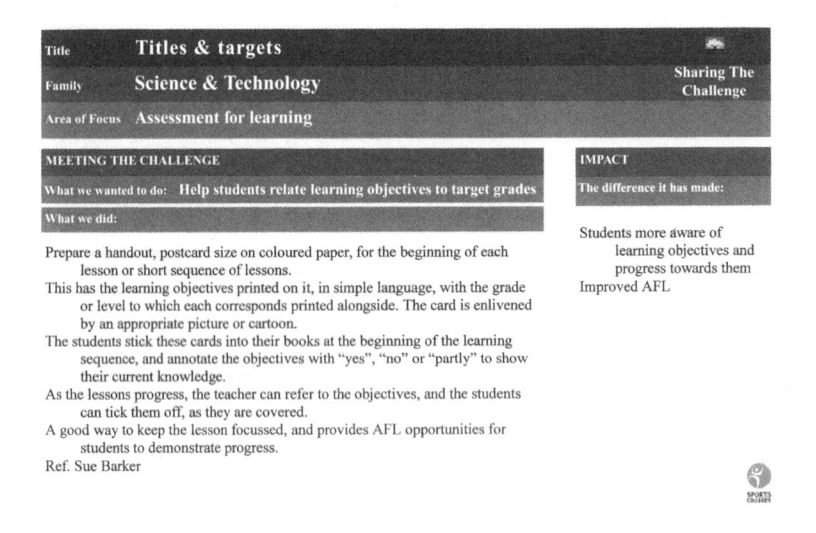

Title	Titles & targets	
Family	Science & Technology	Sharing The Challenge
Area of Focus	Assessment for learning	

MEETING THE CHALLENGE	IMPACT
What we wanted to do: Help students relate learning objectives to target grades	The difference it has made:
What we did:	Students more aware of learning objectives and progress towards them Improved AFL
Prepare a handout, postcard size on coloured paper, for the beginning of each lesson or short sequence of lessons. This has the learning objectives printed on it, in simple language, with the grade or level to which each corresponds printed alongside. The card is enlivened by an appropriate picture or cartoon. The students stick these cards into their books at the beginning of the learning sequence, and annotate the objectives with "yes", "no" or "partly" to show their current knowledge. As the lessons progress, the teacher can refer to the objectives, and the students can tick them off, as they are covered. A good way to keep the lesson focussed, and provides AFL opportunities for students to demonstrate progress. Ref. Sue Barker	

One brick in Northhampton Academy's Wonderwall

Tim and Karen spoke repeatedly about the need to empower students. Tim explained that this can only happen if teachers take seriously what students say and really listen to their views. In turn, to be able to do this, students need to be taught *how* to speak about learning in more serious ways. There have been concerted efforts in the science department to create the breathing space for work on Learning to Learn skills and thinking skills, with the belief that these approaches will equip students with the ability to speak passionately about their learning needs. As part of their mission to inspire learners, high expectations are an important part of every lesson, and Karen explains that she has 'banned the letter t' from her lessons, meaning that students are encouraged to believe in themselves and use the 'can' word rather than 'can't'.

Karen explained that some of her work had been inspired by the notion that all academies have a 'duty to innovate' in order to improve educational outcomes for young people from disadvantaged backgrounds. I would personally be happier if *all* schools felt this duty, irrespective of their circumstances, as young people everywhere deserve the best education they can get. The work of the science department at Northampton Academy shows that using imaginative approaches can help to keep teaching and learning at the cutting edge. But this is just one aspect of the work of the department that is worthy of mention. This work is complemented by a range of other measures that seek to ensure that every individual succeeds. One of the most significant is a rigorous approach to target setting for every student in the department, which is followed up through regular monitoring.

The 'secrets' of success

Having written about the classroom and departmental success of seven individual teachers, it seems timely now to review whether there are any overarching principles that unite those featured.

There appear to be at least seven interrelated success factors that single out these teachers, who have all made a significant difference at the classroom level.

High expectations, high challenge

All seven of the teachers highlighted in this chapter show a passionate commitment to excellence in their classrooms. They expect their students to perform to their potential and—crucially—they design learning experiences that genuinely challenge them. It is noteworthy that some, such as Peter Griffin, are forging ahead with lessons that are challenging students when the prevailing climate in their schools is working in the opposite direction. For teachers to have high expectations in their classrooms, however, they need to have the highest expectations of *themselves* first.

Putting your head above the parapet

Many of the teachers featured have had to emerge from the shadows to tackle classroom challenges head on in their schools. This has required a willingness to answer the difficult questions of critics, as much as it needed the teachers to celebrate any resulting successes. For individual teachers wishing to create change, therefore, there is the need to accept it will not happen if they want to remain anonymous in their schools. The attitude of the teachers featured seems to be that they must get stuck in and do their best to raise standards, even though this will not come without its own difficulties.

Enthusiasm and passion for change

No change would have been possible if the teachers featured had not been hugely passionate about their subject areas and tirelessly enthusiastic as teachers. We cannot expect our students to warm to our lessons if we do not love the subject we teach—enthusiasm is genuinely infectious. This passion is demonstrated by the exciting nature of many of the lessons organised by these teachers, and by the ways they manage to bring their subject areas to life.

Going that extra mile

A key attribute of all the teachers featured was their willingness to put in large amounts of *effort* to get the results they were seeking.

Hard work is far from a new concept for the teaching profession, but in these professionals we see that going the extra mile is the norm for somebody that wants to transform their classroom. I believe that determination and persistence are rather underrated by many people as key criteria for success.

Imaginative approaches

This chapter is replete with unusual, off the wall and creative approaches to teaching and learning that are designed to stop students in their tracks and get them thinking. Only in this way will they be switched on to learning. Planning lessons that inspire in this way takes time, but the teachers featured have clearly repeatedly made this time so they can deliver lessons that really engage students. These imaginative approaches are frequently ideas that the teachers have picked up from others, from a course or from some reading. This in turn indicates the need to be open to new ideas, as well as a willingness to experiment.

Risk taking

Imaginative approaches sometimes work, but they also sometimes flounder. Not everything can work in the classroom, especially if you're trying out a lot of new ideas with a pioneering spirit. The teachers featured in this chapter are clearly not averse to this risk, and indeed some of them seem to revel in it! They show us that by becoming more tolerant of risk, we can sometimes discover untapped reserves of creativity in the classroom. One example is the puppet show Emily Jarvis staged with her year 10 geography students, which might easily have descended into chaos, but actually turned out to be one of the more memorable lessons of the year.

Believing in students, empowering students

The teachers featured clearly respect their students, but they also really believe in them too. Many of the lessons they plan are designed to empower students to *believe* in themselves, to take risks and to work hard towards achieving their potential. It is sometimes difficult to do this when confronted with challenging behaviour or low aspirations but the teachers in this chapter strive to look beyond these initial barriers, so that all students can enjoy success.

How transferable is this work?

The success factors outlined above could easily be included as the key attributes of effective teachers, raising the aspirations of those early in their careers, for example. The key point here is that they are surely not attributes that we think should be rare in schools today. As such, the successes of the teachers featured should be transferable to other schools—providing other teachers are prepared to rise to the challenge. High expectations of themselves should, perhaps, be the place to start.

The successes achieved by the teachers and departments discussed in this chapter should sound a note of hope for those readers who feel that they are rather isolated as they work for positive change in their schools. Thanks to the efforts of those teachers featured, their schools are clearly heading for a much better future, even though there are challenges ahead in spreading the success more widely among staff.

Significantly, the case studies here show that it is possible to create a powerful force for change in a school by making progress at the departmental and classroom level. There are many examples, including some from institutions in which I have worked, of schools facing very challenging circumstances, which have been led to a more optimistic future by the efforts of individual teachers and heads of department. Sometimes it seems that what is required is a 'driver' or innovator, or somebody with the confidence and conviction to try new approaches, who can demonstrate how things *can* be done differently—and successfully. These people can then provide a platform on which others can build, and the justification that it is worth building there too. Success can breed success and doubters can become converts as the culture in the school begins to shift. Staff then start to speak of 'can' or 'could' rather than 'can't', rather like the students in Karen Faulkner's classes.

It is worth noting here that the earlier case studies of whole school success mirror exactly this kind of model of progress—they are certainly not examples of schools that have achieved uniform success across all subject areas and classrooms. Indeed, it could be argued that had they not had a dynamic team driving the school forward by working in *specific* areas, then they would themselves have struggled to achieve the success they have enjoyed. Remember too that success can be fragile, and that a school constantly needs risk-takers and innovators so that it can respond to changing circumstances and new priorities. The topic of drivers for educational change is taken up further in the next chapter, in which I review the overall lessons learnt from the schools featured in the book.

Chapter 8

Learning the Lessons

> 'In order to discover new oceans we need to leave behind familiar shores.' Javis Hayes

In the preceding chapters of the book I've told the stories of schools that have achieved success in at least one aspect of their work. Also featured are teachers and middle leaders who have been successful at a finer scale in their schools. I want to emphasise once again here that the schools featured are not exceptionally privileged institutions enjoying unique advantages. They were not chosen to be included because they represent examples of what can be achieved through rigorous control of the student intake, huge resources, overwhelming parental support or some other special characteristic. They were selected because, in my view, they show what is possible in 'normal' schools and classrooms. And critically, they also show us how success can sometimes be born out of challenging circumstances. In this chapter I want to summarise what I think we have learnt from them, as well as considering what barriers are preventing more schools from enjoying similar success.

To produce this book I spent two years finding diverse examples of successful schools and classrooms in a variety of settings and documenting what was achieved. I have reported, as faithfully as I can, the testimonies of teachers and school leaders in the featured schools. My belief is that they represent a powerful expression of what is possible in schools today and I'm convinced that there's much we can learn from them.

In this chapter, I first want to take the opportunity to reflect on the big picture, having spoken to hundreds of staff and students in the schools featured. In particular, I am eager to unravel any common strands which underpin success—principles which can be used by others to build a brighter future in their own schools. While this falls short of a mechanistic blueprint for success, my hope is that by analysing what the featured schools have done to achieve their goals some meaningful generalised conclusions *can* be drawn. In doing so, I challenge you to consider what others have said in this book about their schools, and to reflect on the relevance of their stories to your own circumstances. There is an exciting opportunity here to consider what has worked in the featured schools and use these principles to help bring you success in your own setting.

Drawing the strands together

I believe there are a number of factors which *all* successful schools seem to have in common that equate to a potential overarching framework for success in schools. I have categorised them below according to five themes: leadership, vision and purpose, culture, people and operational factors. Taken together, these represent the *universal* messages that have emerged from my visits to the schools featured and my conversations with key individuals in these schools, whatever their particular focus when they were visited. They can be seen as interconnected pieces in the jigsaw that constitutes successful schools.

The five domains of successful schools

Domain 1: Leadership

Success is much more likely if leaders, most notably the headteacher, play their full role in the transformation of their schools. They should inspire staff and encourage people to make positive changes on behalf of the school. In particular, leaders should:

- Be committed to continual improvement and the belief that the journey is never over
- Have the highest of expectations of all staff and encourage staff to have high expectations of themselves

- Help all staff to focus on the core mission of the school
- Invest resources and time in staff
- Value all staff and encourage them to value themselves
- Be role models for the behaviours and changes they want to see in the school
- Provide the conditions that allow staff to innovate, develop and thrive
- Celebrate school successes and encourage everyone to have pride in their school
- Be able to see the bigger picture of how their school fits into the wider world

I believe that effective leadership is the most important factor of all in determining whether schools are successful, because leaders can exert a very powerful influence on the remaining four domains for successful schools, as outlined below.

Domain 2: Vision and purpose

Schools need to be clear where they're heading and why this is important. In schools that make effective use of this sense of vision and purpose, the following appear particularly important:

- An overall vision is agreed collectively, with individuals innovating to achieve specific goals
- Staff and students are aware of the school's vision and work together as a community to make it a reality
- Staff are united behind a common cause, with a shared understanding of its relevance to students' lives and the long-term benefits it brings
- Key people are aware of what actions need to be taken to move things forward—an overarching, but not restrictive, strategy is in place to do this
- There is a clarity of purpose focused firmly on the development and care of students as *individuals*, whose effort is celebrated as much as any academic achievements
- The school is aware of its wider role in the community and takes steps to develop a 'learning community'

Domain 3: Culture

The prevailing culture in any institution is key to it achieving its goals. If there is a distinctive culture in successful schools, then it would appear to encompass at least the following elements:

- Everyone is valued
- Belief that high expectations underpin everything that is done in school
- Belief that hard work, dedication and perseverance count a great deal in education
- A recognition that creative approaches can have powerful results
- A willingness to take risks
- An openness to new ideas and approaches
- Key stakeholders providing their active support for the things that matter
- Happiness, security and well-being of staff and students is a key cornerstone of the work of the school

Domain 4: People

Success is only possible if there are people who are able to drive forward changes and carry out key actions. The following are especially important:

- 'Drivers' are needed to drive innovation forward and provide a catalyst for change—from the classroom to the whole school level
- All staff should feel able to step forward to act as a catalyst for the changes they feel passionately about
- Staff should have the ability to deliver change through their knowledge, skills and attributes
- Individuals take responsibility for their own professional development, learning from the latest developments
- Staff should understand that they need to play their full part in delivering change by carrying out specific actions themselves
- Small teams should take the lead to address key challenges

- Staff should recognise that they work as a whole staff team as well as in small teams
- People need to breathe life into written policies, plans and protocols

Domain 5: Operational factors

Success can only be achieved if operational factors allow positive changes to be implemented. Within successful schools, the following seem especially crucial:

- Effective systems (plans, policies, protocols) are set up that get things done
- Support staff are channelled into areas of priority need
- 'Smart' use of people and budgets is used to fast track the school to success
- The projects that deliver change fit with local priorities
- Additional resources are dedicated to the projects delivering change
- Enterprising approaches are used to put the school on a more business-like footing

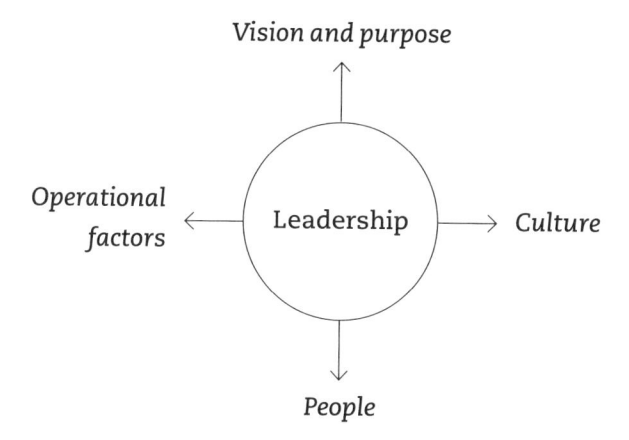

The five domains of successful schools

Individual departments and classrooms

While the major part of the book is taken up with testimonies from school leaders and teachers which chart whole school successes, I reserved Chapter 7 for stories of change at the departmental and classroom level. I wanted to explore the extent to which positive change and success can thrive at a finer scale in a school, even though the wider school community may not be recognised for innovative work. The impressive findings of this chapter are that success *can* flourish—often somewhat hidden—within individual departments and classrooms, and that this can provide the catalyst for more profound whole school success, *if* leaders recognise, celebrate and build on this success. The worst case scenario, however, is that not only is this success not recognised outside the school, but it is overlooked within it too.

Recent studies in the performance of schools have suggested that within school variation is as significant, and is sometimes more significant, than variation between schools. This clearly has serious implications for the evidence that is used to judge whether a school is providing good value for money or whether parents should choose to send their children there. It also suggests that, where schools are struggling to implement positive change, 'oases' of good practice could be used as a springboard for wider, whole school measures.

Finding and managing the 'right' people

Throughout the book the vital role of people in creating the changes necessary for schools to succeed is highlighted time and time again. For that reason, *people* were included as one of the five themes of successful schools. One of the aims of the book, however, was to include some general principles which others can build on in their own schools. For this reason I've tried to identify at the end of each chapter the systemic factors that appear to have brought success to the schools featured, as well as the role of key people. Linked to this is the idea of the *transferability* of the work carried out in each school too, a topic which is also touched upon at the end of each case study. Together, this information is intended to empower other school leaders as they wrestle with their day to day challenges, rather than thinking that they simply have to find the 'right' people to take the lead.

It would be unfair, however, to pretend that you can simply set up appropriate systems and protocols in your school and success will naturally flow from this. One of the most powerful messages that comes from the schools featured is that key individuals *do* provide the catalyst for positive change in schools, as well as the passion and energy to carry through innovations and projects to successful completion. Such individuals are perhaps best termed 'drivers', and I want to devote some space here to considering how you can find, nurture and manage such drivers in your own school. Without them, I've no doubt that progress will be much slower than you would like.

What are the characteristics of drivers?

I want to clarify first the key attributes, skills and knowledge of drivers—the things that mark them out as people who can fast track a school to success. This is partly so the character of drivers can be defined and partly so school leaders can learn to spot such people among their staff. Note that drivers do not have to be teachers—support staff are equally able to fulfil the role.

Characteristics of a driver

The following characteristics tend to be exhibited by drivers. Note that early in their careers people are less likely to display these characteristics in abundance, or may be yet to develop some of them.

Attributes

- High levels of energy
- Infectiously enthusiastic
- Optimistic
- Doggedly persistent
- Hard working

- Very much committed to making a difference
- Possessing a real passion for a particular development
- A child-centred attitude to all their work

Skills

- Able to form a clear vision of where they're heading and why
- Able to think up creative solutions to challenges and problems
- Able to think on their feet
- Excellent at networking

Knowledge

- Knows what needs to be done to achieve goals
- Knows how the 'system' works that will bring success
- Has specialist knowledge relevant to challenge being faced

Do you want all staff to be drivers?

One of the important principles that emerged from the case studies in this book is that whole school change takes place due to changes that take root at a finer level—in departments and classrooms for example. As such, successful schools are surely places where all staff feel empowered to act as drivers when appropriate, bringing success to areas of practice that need to be improved. Teachers should, therefore, be willing and able to act as drivers in their own classrooms to get the best for their students. By doing so, they will help to drive up standards across the whole school. While they may fall short of acting as whole school drivers, their work at the classroom level is, nevertheless, significant as schools strive for success.

How do you find whole school drivers?

If drivers play a significant role in school change, then it seems sensible to be able spot these talented people as early as possible.

They can then be nurtured and supported to create maximum benefit for the school. It needs to be said straight away that given time any whole school driver should reveal themselves by being the creative force behind at least one important new development at your school. These are not people who are usually comfortable staying in the shadows for long! However, it may be that teachers early in their careers are leading small scale change in their classrooms that is not recognised by school leaders. Given encouragement, such people may soon be leading whole school initiatives that create more widespread change. If they are serious about finding drivers schools should, therefore, at every level be on the lookout for people who could become whole school drivers. Being open to what colleagues are achieving is vital, as is some sort of formalised system for passing on examples of good practice to leaders.

How do you manage whole school drivers?

Once identified, drivers need to be managed effectively in order to ensure their efforts are maximised. School leaders need to think carefully about the needs of drivers and ensure they carry out a range of measures to ensure they feel supported. They also should recognise that drivers can sometimes lack strategic oversight of the school's priorities and occasionally need to be reined in. This is a difficult balance, as it is vital not to allow them to feel that they are stifled. Some practical measures can clearly make a real difference here in managing drivers effectively.

Managing your drivers

- Cherish them as individuals
- Recognise that their idiosyncrasies may add to their creative strength
- Put a solid support network behind them to share the workload
- Ensure that they meet with key people on a regular basis to update others

- Encourage them to have big ideas, but help them to ground these in the reality of day to day school life
- Make it clear that while all ideas are valid, leaders will need to prioritise what comes first

How do you provide the conditions for all staff to become whole school drivers?

The spirit of education is that everybody is developing and learning all the time. This means that while any individual member of staff in your school may not currently feel comfortable being a whole school driver, they are *capable* of developing the characteristics to take on such a role. While some of the attributes, skills and knowledge of drivers are clearly harder to acquire than others (optimism and passion are, for example, hard to *learn*), it would be a very pessimistic view of personal development to write oneself off completely. So the key message here is that if the school works hard to provide an appropriate climate to allow staff to develop into whole school drivers, then colleagues *can* grow into the role. Several examples in the book bear witness to this, with individuals stepping out from the shadows to be the creative force behind changes that they were especially passionate about.

While it would be nice to think that all schools strive to provide the conditions for *all* staff to develop the capacity to become whole school drivers, this is clearly not the case. Unfortunately, in some schools or departments the ethos does not always encourage such people to thrive, as new ideas are not welcomed or leaders are too concerned with their own status to bring up and coming talent into the fold. To counter this, and provide some practical suggestions for school leaders on how you can grow your own drivers, I include below some principles that can be implemented in any school.

Growing your own drivers

- Believe in all staff and show you value them
- Make it clear to staff that leaders do not always have the right answers
- Encourage experimentation and creative approaches
- Organise Continuing Professional Development opportunities that complement an innovative approach to education
- Nurture anybody willing to take the initiative as a driver
- Reassure drivers that a team will help them to move things forward (ensure that you genuinely mean this!)
- Devote resources to initiatives that really matter to the school, including people
- Celebrate the successes of all staff

What about external drivers?

The example of the Dearne Valley Education Partnership (Chapter 6) showed us that we sometimes need to harness the skills of a driver who is *external* to our school in order to achieve improved outcomes within the institution. Other examples have shown that working with external partners often brings us into contact with people who are able to influence and direct change in our schools, even if they are not leading such developments. The message is that within schools we need to be open to the role that these external drivers can play in school improvement. We also need to harness their skills and knowledge, and when recruiting people to lead collaborative projects, be aware that those from outside our school often bring with them additional benefits and insights. As schools engage with extended services and look towards new and exciting forms of formal collaboration with other institutions and local services, the importance of these external drivers is likely to grow.

Should headteachers be drivers?

Finally, we turn to the concept of whether headteachers themselves need to be drivers in their schools. It should quickly become clear that the characteristics of a driver, as outlined above, include many factors which are also vital to effective school leadership. Indeed, it could be argued that being a driver is about taking on a leadership role in the school for a specific initiative, whatever your status. As such, headteachers should be ideally placed to be drivers in their schools. The school case studies in this book show many examples of headteachers acting as drivers in their schools, and it would seem that the ability to drive forward in this way with positive change is an essential attribute of any headteacher.

Headteachers are not always able to take the lead, however, and ideally need a team of people who provide drive for particular initiatives. While these may be people who step forward as drivers under their own initiative, they could equally be colleagues who have key responsibilities delegated to them—'named drivers' if you like—that allow the headteacher to retain the strategic overview. As such headteachers should also be able to provide a framework in which change can occur, while not always making that change happen themselves. Sometimes, however, headteachers need people to flag up issues that are not currently on their radar, but which are nevertheless central to school improvement.

If schools are going to be really effective institutions then I believe that these drivers should not be the same people all the time; rather there should be different members of staff stepping forward to act as drivers when their skills or passion for the topic make them ideal candidates. If a school is able to create this ethos of distributed leadership, then it is surely best placed to achieve its goals more quickly.

Chapter 8: Learning the Lessons | 219

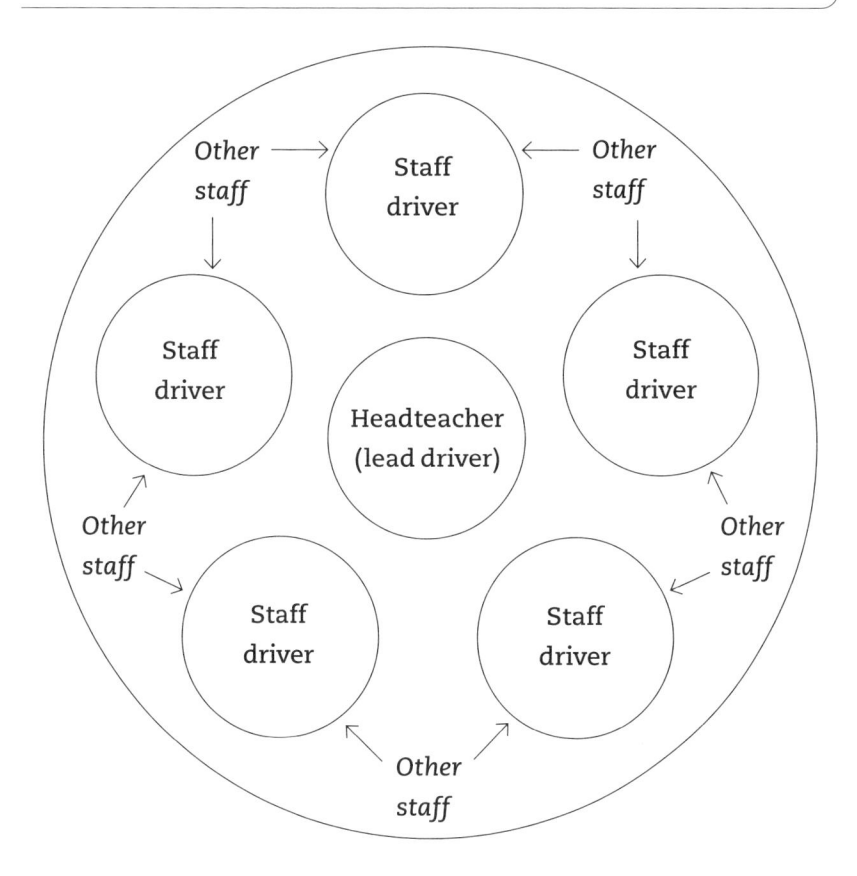

Effective schools need a variety of staff to play their role as drivers for change

If you are a headteacher and feel you are not currently providing the drive you would like for your school, it may be worth considering the characteristics of drivers in more detail. Having interviewed a lot of headteachers for the purposes of this book, I feel that for some headteachers the key area that needs to be developed is the *creative* dimension of school leadership. The good news is that there are some excellent courses and books to engage with that can help you develop your creativity as a school leader.

The final point I wish to emphasise about headteachers is that, having reviewed carefully the information gathered for this book, there is no doubt that they represent a very powerful force for positive change in schools. Perhaps this is an obvious point but it does need to be stated. If you currently work in a school that is struggling to move forward, then the quality of leadership will inevitably come under the spotlight. My belief, more generally—and this is certainly borne out by the examples in this book—is that the success of schools is directly proportional to the quality of leadership of headteachers.

Surprise findings

While many of the findings from the book resonated with my own thoughts on the factors contributing to the success of schools, gained from fifteen years working in and supporting schools, some things came as a surprise. The next section deals with these somewhat unexpected yet serendipitous findings.

Strategy

My assumption before beginning this book was that schools that are successful cannot achieve this success without meticulous *planning*. However, several of the schools featured have highlighted the fact that the key developments that enabled them to achieve their goals seem to have happened by chance—or at most have been opportunities that the schools have grasped at the right moment. This has led me to consider carefully the degree to which a clear *strategy* is important to successful schools.

In educational terms, a strategy is usually understood to be a plan of action that will achieve a particular outcome—a plan that also sets out who will be doing what, the rationale for the work and a timeline for events. Within this definition there are clearly a variety of ways of articulating a strategy, including the degree to which it is *prescribed* and the detail of the actions that will help the school achieve its goals. My belief is that while the schools featured in the book have correctly established that their success sometimes seems to have arisen out of chance opportunities, all would also say that an overarching master plan was guiding actions on a day to day basis. Indeed it was this master plan—or the vision that underpinned it—that enabled somebody at the school to recognise that an opportunity could help the school move forward towards its preferred future. In this way a kind of organic development was possible.

The key message about strategy appears to be, therefore, that it should be in place but should not be so restrictive that it does not allow for flexibility to adapt to changing circumstances, and indeed to allow schools to grasp attractive—if perhaps unplanned or unforeseen—opportunities. The ability to take risks and be enterprising in the face of opportunities are two important factors here.

Monitoring and evaluation

We're living in times when any educational initiative that does not include Monitoring and Evaluation in capital letters seems doomed to failure. But the stories of the schools in the book tell otherwise. While these two activities—monitoring to judge progress and evaluating to determine quality—were clearly built into the work of the schools featured in this book, their detailed testimonies signal a much more relaxed view of monitoring and evaluation than I was expecting. While some of this was clearly down to the skill of key people to spot and rectify problems without having rigorous procedures in place, I could not escape the somewhat controversial conclusion that monitoring and evaluation—especially in an administratively heavy form—could be just a little overrated as a tool for school improvement. Having said this I do believe that when schools are *struggling* to achieve success, then monitoring and evaluation can reveal information which is useful in charting a path towards a brighter future.

The barriers to innovation

The first part of this chapter was unswervingly upbeat in tone as I tried to identify and celebrate the factors that have contributed to the success of the schools featured in this book. My hope, on beginning this project, was that the book would provide an optimistic study of all things good about school-based education in the first decade of the twenty-first century. However, as the book started to take shape, I realised that I needed to explore the reasons why the kinds of innovation highlighted are not as commonplace as we would wish them to be in our schools. In this second part of the chapter, therefore, I wish to explore in more detail the barriers to innovation in our schools. I am eager to outline what I think can be done at the national and local level to empower school leaders and teachers towards success—something which I do in the final chapter. But in order to do so it is necessary to explore first what is currently hindering schools from embracing the approaches that could bring them success. I will begin this chapter with a failed project of my own that taught me something profound about schools.

> 'If you believe you can or believe you can't you're right.' Walt Disney

Seeking out innovation

I first launched the School Innovation Awards in 2004 in order to stimulate, celebrate and reward creative (i.e. new and appropriate) practice in schools across the UK. I was keen to put something back into schools from the modest profits of my company in the form of small cash prizes of £500. My experience is that such sums of money can provide the catalyst for real change in schools—enabling the building blocks for the kinds of projects featured in the book to be laid. My vision was that the awards would encourage schools to launch a range of small scale creative projects of their own in order to improve educational opportunities. I backed up the scheme with some high profile advertising in educational publications and personally told hundreds of school leaders and teachers about the awards in the course of my work. I was keen to encourage as many schools as possible to apply and was looking forward to spending time sifting through some high quality entries. I had purposefully made the application process simple and straightforward in order to encourage schools to apply.

You can imagine my disappointment, therefore, when the deadline for the judging arrived and the pile of entries received was barely thicker than the card folder on which I had optimistically written 'School Innovation Awards' six months earlier. I received only nine applications in 2004 and this figure dwindled further a year later. Reluctantly, I made the decision to end my award scheme after two years due to lack of interest from schools. I had learnt a lesson: most school leaders and teachers do not seem ready to innovate in order to improve, even with cash incentives!

Three years on, I sometimes ponder what precisely it was that made schools feel unable to apply for this additional cash for school improvement. Surely a page of A4 outlining how they wished to develop innovative practice was not too much to ask for? Now that I have more experience of the pervading school attitude towards creative approaches, I realise that I should have readied myself for the small number of entries to my award scheme. Despite the many success stories in this book—and the positive state of mind that has made them possible—I have to admit that the outlook of these schools is not mirrored by the majority of institutions. I consider this a travesty for the young people growing up in them today because I firmly believe that what the schools featured have achieved is within the compass of others. How, I wondered, has it become possible for so many school leaders and teachers to become so disenfranchised from the possibility of change that they overlook such opportunities? The rest of this chapter goes on to consider the barriers to innovation in our schools.

External and internal barriers

Though there are many reasons for the lack of innovative practice in schools, they tend to fall into two categories: factors external to schools and those within them. While no single factor is probably enough in its own right to stem creativity, the combined effect is powerful. It has resulted in a kind of 'firefighting' and coping with the status quo that is all too common in our education system; it has caused many schools to fear change imposed from above, rather than taking ownership and embracing it.

External pressures

A quartet of interrelated factors from outside schools seems to hinder the use of innovative approaches. Many schools have found it hard to release the shackles of a National Curriculum which seems to prescribe so much, yet provide such little time to cover all the content. This forms part of a wider pressure for schools to deliver a government agenda dominated by league tables, testing and exams, which is often seen as being imposed from above with scant regard for local priorities and circumstances.

Unfortunately, this national agenda is so frequently subject to change—most frequently through the now dreaded government 'initiative'—that many schools spend so much time keeping up with the latest changes that they feel there is little time to develop fresh and meaningful approaches of their own. Most worryingly, these approaches are often precisely what need to be introduced in order for the school to become more effective. Lastly, the financial uncertainties affecting many schools encourage them to stay on safe ground rather than taking bold steps into the unknown.

School challenges

The heavy climate of prescription in schools over the last decade has resulted in another, often insidious, problem. Many school leaders, teachers and parents have begun to accept the prevailing government view of the goals of education and methods that should be used to attain them—even though there are stark ethical conflicts lurking beneath the surface. In short, *personal* vision about what is really important in education has become something of a rarity. And rarer still is a clear articulation, as a school community, of what this vision *really* stands for and why this is important, one that goes far beyond the bland and ubiquitous 'off the shelf' values and aims document which adorns many school prospectuses, but is ignored by many staff.

External pressures

Schools find it hard to release the shackles of the National Curriculum

School challenges

There is often a lack of understanding of creativity and its relevance across the curriculum

Teachers/school leaders often lack the skills to teach for and using creativity

Disempowered staff and students find it hard to embrace creativity

So learning and teaching for creativity is not valued or developed in many schools

Schools feel pressured to deliver government's agenda for education

Constant change in education leaves schools feeling they have little time to develop fresh approaches

Financial pressures encourage schools to stay on safe ground

The barriers to creative practice in our schools

The result is that many schools feel pulled and stretched in all sorts of ways, according to *other people's* visions of what they should be doing. In many schools, there is often also a lack of understanding of what creative approaches can really achieve—something this book hopes to address. While this sometimes can be addressed through empowerment, it also requires the acquisition of new skills and a determination to be positive and optimistic about the possibilities for change. Unless staff are engaged in the process, it is easy for them to become disempowered and disenchanted, meaning it is virtually impossible for them to try out new approaches.

The ways in which these factors may interrelate is shown in the diagram on the previous page. It suggests that the combined pressure results in truly creative approaches simply not being valued or developed in many schools. Indeed, it seems to be feared in many schools through concerns over what might go wrong.

The implications for students

The fact that creative approaches are not cherished and nurtured in many schools is a problem in its own right. However, when one considers the implications for students, it is clear that urgent action will need to be taken if we are to fully prepare these young people for the uncertain world of tomorrow. If school leaders and teachers are not modelling the creative process in their own work, how can they be expected to nurture creative problem-solving skills or responsibility in their students? Creativity is emerging as a key life skill for everyone, allowing people to find solutions and so thrive in the future. We cannot afford to let the current generation of school age children miss out.

I would not want these barriers to success to leave readers feeling too pessimistic about what can be achieved in schools—this is not what the book is for. Indeed, there is much we can do to help schools achieve success and in the final chapter I will consider what *can* be done at the school, government and societal level so that more schools can say 'We did it here!'

Chapter 9

A Manifesto for Real Change in our Schools

> *'Be the change you want to see in the world.'* Mahatma Gandhi

Wouldn't it be wonderful if you could throw caution to the wind and outline what you think really needs to be done to create meaningful change in our schools? Change that would allow substantially more schools to enjoy success in the way that those institutions featured in the book have done. Over the last few years I've had this urge quite a few times and have mulled over the first few elements of my manifesto on numerous occasions. Time has prevented me from going much further. Now that I've had the luxury of thinking and writing in detail about successful schools, the final chapter seems like a logical place for me to articulate in detail my personal 'manifesto for real change' in our schools. The aim is to suggest what needs to be done to provide the conditions for many more schools to achieve success and say 'We did it here too!' As the previous chapter has shown, there are significant barriers to innovation in our schools that seem to be preventing many—perhaps the majority—from creating the kind of brighter future for young people that they would wish for. The purpose of any manifesto for educational change should surely be to remove these barriers and help schools to achieve their dreams.

As I began to think more fully about how schools can enjoy wider success, I realised that three different parties—schools, government (local and national) and wider society—all have a role to play in creating the conditions for positive change in education. I believe there are ten fronts on which we should be operating, and I outline below what I see as the critical areas that need to be addressed. I also try to clarify some actions that each party needs to carry out to play its part, and then consider where I believe the majority influence lies. Finally, I end the book by considering the implications of the manifesto for various individuals and groups.

1. **School leaders will be skilled in leadership and teaching and learning in equal proportion**

A national debate is currently taking place over the skills needed for school leadership following concern over the scarcity of senior managers in schools who are prepared to progress into the most senior positions. While some radical new models have been proposed—including the idea that future headteachers may not have come from a traditional teaching background at all—one constant is that future school leaders will need to be skilled in organisational leadership and teaching and learning in equal proportion. While the skills needed for each of these are rather distinct, we need to find ways of ensuring that school leaders of the future are fully equipped to lead modern, forward looking—and most crucially of all—innovative schools. Schools are complex, multifaceted organisations, with budgets often topping £10 million annually for the largest secondaries. They need strong leadership but also require somebody at the helm who understands intimately the teaching and learning process. That is, after all, what schools are about. The excellent work of the National College for School Leadership (NCSL) in this area needs to be built upon, and at every level we need to make a concerted effort to find and nurture the next generation of school leaders.

Schools can play their part by recognising the need for strong organisational leadership skills

This requires school leaders to engage with programmes that allow them to learn from other sectors, such as the Partners in Leadership programme offered by the organisation Business in the Community. It also requires school leaders and governors to value more highly the input of the business community, senior leaders from other sectors and other key professionals. School leaders' knowledge on the latest findings from educational research must also be kept current—for example, through their scrutiny of the superb publications of the National Foundation for Educational Research (NFER).

The government can play its part by creating the support structures for the next generation of school leaders

The work of the NCSL should be built upon and extended to ensure that there is a rigorous support network in place for school leaders. More programmes to link schools with businesses and the wider world outside schools should be introduced, and the government should provide support for school leaders taking sabbaticals to learn from other sectors. The government should also be more open to the appointment of people with the appropriate skills to lead schools who have not come from traditional teaching backgrounds.

Wider society can play its part by campaigning for and supporting a new generation of school leaders who are appropriately skilled

Parents can do this by asking about the leadership training of key staff in schools, and for details of the school's collaborative work with business and other sectors. For their own part, businesses need to make efforts to link with schools, and business leaders should commit time to programmes and other support work which will allow school leaders to learn more about the world outside the school gates. Business people who are involved in strategic work in their companies are especially well placed to support this aspect of work in schools.

2. School leaders and teachers will be trusted as highly trained professionals

Despite extensive prequalification training and ongoing professional development, for some reason we seem to find it hard as a nation to trust teachers and school leaders to carry out their role as highly trained professionals—as people who can make discerning choices about what they teach, how they teach it and the whole school systems that will help create success. Since the introduction of the National Curriculum, we've seen the autonomy of educational professionals reduced, and worse still have begun to see a new generation of teachers who expect to be *told* what to do, rather than use their professional judgement to find appropriate solutions to the challenges that face them. We cannot create an outstanding education system if teachers see themselves as robots that need to be programmed; as deliverers of 'content'; as people who simply prepare youngsters for tests and examinations. Instead, we need to rediscover our respect for education professionals. If we can do that then they can be allowed not only to dream about creating a brighter future for young people, but start working towards that vision, unhindered, tomorrow.

Schools can play their part by standing up for the professionalism of teachers and leaders

This will only be convincing if teachers and school leaders have the highest of expectations of themselves and are committed to staying up to date with key knowledge and skills. This means that they need to develop their own distinctive pedagogies for teaching that are appropriate to local circumstances, rather than relying on 'quick and dirty' off the shelf teaching approaches. It also means they need to develop a more enlightened view of Continuing Professional Development (CPD) opportunities, including where and when training events take place. It requires teachers to accept that the best learning takes place with appropriate planning and feedback to learners—and this all takes *quality* time. If people in wider society are to trust schools more, then schools also need to be more open, encouraging others to find out about their work. This should extend beyond open days and special events—an 'open door' policy, with appropriate safety controls, should be introduced so that the work of schools can be demystified.

The government can play its part by respecting the autonomy of education professionals

Accountability in schools is vital, but the government's recent focus on control has brought Big Brother-like overtones to our education system, stifling individual expression. By moving away from this in favour of allowing teachers and schools to find local solutions to local issues, the government can help teachers and leaders to regain the professionalism they deserve. The government can also support teachers in acquiring new skills and knowledge through a more strategic view of the role of CPD—for example, by guaranteeing teachers more time to attend courses and engage in other development activities.

Wider society can play its part by trusting teachers and school leaders as highly trained professionals

Too many people still think that teaching is a cushy job—with short hours, decent pay and long holidays. People can educate themselves about what life is *really* like in schools by spending time seeing them at work. This includes learning about the real working week of teachers and school leaders. Those who are already convinced about the professionalism of teachers can help by encouraging others not to question teaching pedagogy simply because they've spent several years as a student in a school. Rather like doctors being experts in healing, we need to trust our teachers as experts in learning.

3. An overall framework to help schools succeed will be provided, but this will also allow them to innovate to find appropriate local solutions

If we are to prepare young people for the uncertainties of tomorrow then we cannot go back to the educationally liberal 1960s, when experimentation in the classroom went into orbit. Schools need a clear overall framework in which they should work, one that outlines the core knowledge, skills and attributes that teachers and school leaders should strive to develop in their students. But vitally, this framework must not be so prescriptive as to strangle the creativity out of schools. They must be allowed to take controlled risks, to innovate and to experiment within this framework, with the aim of finding new and better ways to achieve their goals. They must be allowed to use approaches that have a better fit with local circumstances. I believe we are at last starting to see a move towards this new model as the revised National Curriculum, with inherent flexibility, comes into effect. It cannot come soon enough.

Schools can play their part in accepting the need for an overall national framework for their work

It is unrealistic for schools in the maintained sector to think that education can be a completely blank canvas—overarching guidelines on what is taught in schools are key to this accountable public body. The freedom that the new National Curriculum will bring, however, means that they need to accept the additional *responsibility* for making autonomous decisions about what is taught and the methods that are used. It seems that some schools are still a little afraid of this responsibility. Appropriate decisions will be made only if schools become more skilled at designing curricula that genuinely engage and inspire students—and this needs conviction as much as it needs additional training.

The government can play its part by providing flexibility within our education system for schools—thankfully this is finally starting to happen

The revised National Curriculum with its exciting new cross-curricular themes looks set to inject a long overdue element of flexibility into the education system in England. This should be built upon in examination and test syllabuses in a way that allows teachers to teach concepts, key ideas and theories as much as facts to be regurgitated. The government can also help by recognising more formally through the curriculum the factors that are harder to measure in schools, especially the social and emotional development of children and young people.

Wider society can play its part by lobbying government for a more locally responsive education system

This can be done as much by individual parents as it can through groups such as the National Federation of Parent Teacher Organisations. Individuals can also help by offering their skills and knowledge to schools to allow them to offer more exciting curricula, infused with real life examples that are relevant to students' lives. This can form part of a more concerted effort by parents to encourage schools to devise locally relevant curricula.

4. We will let go of the notion that continual, short-term change is beneficial to schools and learners

One of the things that most frustrates teachers and school leaders is the climate of constant, short-term—and often short-sighted—change that has pervaded schools over the last decade. While it is true that in any complex system change is to be expected, and we all need to develop ways to embrace its potential more warmly, the pace of change in the education world is bewildering. Headteachers' desks will even today be piled high with government documents outlining the latest initiatives, all of which require training and resources. This obsession with change is in part surely a result of our electoral system, which places an imperative on governments to demonstrate 'progress' within ridiculously short timescales. We cannot let education become, curiously, a victim of democracy. But how can we move away from this continual change agenda in our schools? In short, by trusting in a smaller number of meaningful changes that unite teachers, school leaders, students and parents in areas that are truly worth working towards. This will require faith by voters—especially parents—as much as it will require vision from politicians. It will also require an acceptance from schools that new priorities do emerge that need to be tackled.

Schools can play their part by accepting that change is inevitable, while being discerning about which changes they are prepared to accept

Schools can become more robust to externally imposed changes by developing and articulating their own vision. Sadly, this is a much neglected area in many schools which often—mistakenly—equate their school improvement plan with a vision. Only with a clearly articulated vision can schools make more discerning choices about which government initiatives they are prepared to embrace. Governors have a key role in this vision building process in schools too. Schools must be responsive to changing circumstances. School leaders and teachers must also be mindful that there are many examples of issues that have serious implications for schools (childhood obesity or violent crime, for example) that simply cannot be ignored and are fully merited in being the focus of new government initiatives.

The government can play its part by creating more stability within the education system and introducing only those initiatives that will really make a difference

The pace of change within the education system does at last seem to be slowing down. Now that the brakes are on, the government should take this opportunity to consider which long-term changes will really make a difference in schools. They should convene an independent group to look into this issue, which will seek to gain a wide spectrum of views on what society really values in our schools. This should form the basis of a robust long-term vision and strategy for education in this country in the twenty-first century. The government must also be bold not to jump at new opportunities to impose short-term changes on schools for purely political reasons—and this in turn requires a more ethical approach to government.

Wider society can play its part by encouraging the government and schools to trust in meaningful long-term changes

Voters can exert a powerful force on the government by giving their support to politicians who are committed to meaningful long-term changes in education. But voters first need to pause to consider the changes they believe are needed—to build their own vision for our education system based on their values and beliefs. Parents can support schools by encouraging their work to address local issues, rather than perceived national priorities highlighted by government. They should hold back from making decisions about where to send their children until a more rounded view has been gained of what schools can offer—one that goes beyond a slavish following of national agendas.

5. *We will accept that the national obsession with tests, targets and examinations is not producing learners with the knowledge and skills to thrive in the uncertain world of tomorrow*

From the age of 4 up until the time teenagers leave compulsory education they are bombarded by a raft of tests, targets and examinations that would exhaust many adults. Indeed, I would go as far as saying that there is a national obsession with tests in our country—fuelled in part by high profile media events aimed at 'testing the nation' or putting some other measure on our abilities. The government has done more than its fair share to add fuel to the testing inferno, with so many new tests that teachers sometimes feel that there is precious little time for much else. Despite all this testing the UK continually scores poorly on many measures of academic and other performance of its students compared to their European and North American counterparts. This suggests that the testing obsession is simply not getting the intended results. Perhaps most worryingly of all, the UK's children and young people are currently plagued by record levels of stress, depression and other psychological illnesses—one of the factors that no doubt contributed to the country's recent bottom placing in a childhood happiness poll conducted by UNESCO.

The view from government seems to be that the 'high tide' of this testing culture *has* been reached, but equally its 'tide mark' has left a lasting legacy in schools. We must first accept that the current barrage of tests is not conducive to children's well-being, while standing up for the skills and knowledge that will prepare them for the future. At the same time we need to recognise that it can be hard to measure the things that really matter in schools. In short, we need to demonstrate that schools are places of learning not testing.

Schools can play their part by engaging with only those tests and targets that really matter, while accepting that they need to be accountable for what they do

Schools that put great emphasis on their place in the 'league table' of results are not helping parents to judge schools as rounded institutions. Some schools go even further by getting involved in a whole barrage of additional tests and exams, which are then used as headline grabbers in school literature. While examination and test results are clearly important, they are not the *only* measures against which we should judge successful schools. Schools should also be champions of the wider benefits of education—such as the acquisition by students of key skills to help them live happy and successful lives. They should promote these skills in their prospectuses and they should strive to make them a genuine part of their culture.

The government can play its part by adopting a much less prescriptive view of education testing and targets

England remains one of the few countries in Europe which publicises school exam results as league tables. They have been scrapped in Wales, Scotland and Northern Ireland in recent years, after initially following the English lead. While exam results are obviously important indicators for parents and the government of a school's success, the use of crude league tables implies they are *all* that matters. The government should investigate a much wider range of criteria for judging successful schools and encourage parents to make choices based on a fuller picture of the school. Scrapping education league tables in favour of a more rounded view of a school's success—which genuinely reflects its intake—would be a step in the right direction.

Wider society can play its part by refusing to accept crude measures of academic achievement as the sole means of judging effective schools

We need a national debate about the measures on which we should judge effective schools. This should include discussion of the balance between knowledge and skills, as well as the kind of things children should know about and be able to do when they leave school. It should also deal with the social and emotional aspects of learning. This debate will inform work at the government level to identify some fairer measures on which to judge the success of schools. Parents and others in society need to actively engage with this debate if it is to be successful.

6. We will stand up for what really matters in our schools— creating happy, resourceful and well-educated students equipped with lifelong thinking and learning skills

The raft of government initiatives, tests and targets can often lead us to lose sight of what schools should really be for: giving young people the power to make profound choices in their lives and the resolve to deal with whatever is thrown at them along the way. While such things as literacy, oracy and numeracy clearly matter a great deal, so do personal resourcefulness, thinking skills, learning to learn abilities and the ability to have fun, enjoy one's life and help to make the world a better place. Unless we are, at every level, prepared to stand up for what we think really matters in our schools, then we will always be slavishly following someone else's agenda. Moreover, the people who draw up such agendas may not, sometimes through ignorance rather than design, have the best interests of young people at heart.

Schools can play their part by championing what education should really be for

Many schools make reference to educating the 'whole person' in their values statements, but actions speak louder than words. The result is that academic success is often deemed to be the only measure of success for students. While maintaining their commitment to high academic standards, schools can also celebrate the *effort* of students more systematically. They can also devise specific programmes to help students gain wider skills to be able to thrive in the uncertain world of tomorrow—for example, through enterprise and problem-solving activities. It requires work at many levels before a school is able to say that the education of the whole person is truly part of their ethos.

The government can play its part by setting its sights on higher goals for education

The government's eagerness to demonstrate progress through tests is set against a backdrop of a generation of youngsters whose well-being is precariously balanced. High levels of alcohol and drug abuse, high teenage pregnancy rates, record highs in stress-related illnesses are all worrying truths about young people growing up in Britain today. While these deep-seated social issues are not something that schools can tackle alone, the government can provide hope by appointing a young person's 'Happiness Tsar'. This person would work to address the well-being of children, and their work would cover the remit of schools to improve quality of life for students—including the acquisition of key life skills.

Wider society can play its part by standing up for what schools should be striving for

Parents can make a difference by asking probing questions about schools' work at the social and emotional level, in addition to their concerns about academic matters. They should hold back from criticising the 'soft' subjects of citizenship and Personal, Social and Health Education (PSHE), as these views are not informed by the powerful research evidence showing the wider benefits of such education for students. They can also pause more generally to consider what really matters in their children's—and their own—lives.

7. Schools will learn from each other, and from the wider world, in order to avoid 'institutionalised' thinking

Collaborative work *between* schools has curiously not been a traditional feature of our education system, beyond the occasional special event or sporting fixtures. The result is a kind of 'institutionalised' thinking that is not apparent to educational professionals until they leave the immediate institution in which they've been working. This can be damaging to students, as it often results in blinkered thinking about what can or cannot work, limited ambition based on past failures or a reluctance to consider new approaches that are considered 'unworkable' in a particular school. While school culture can exert a tremendously positive force on an institution, it can also stifle creativity and create a climate where experimentation is frowned upon, with those who have been in the school for years 'knowing best'. We must tackle this issue head on by encouraging much more systematic cross-working between schools and outside the education sector, in order to celebrate and share good practice and lift expectations. While the government can do much to facilitate this change, it is teachers and school leaders who must be prepared to step forward if it is to work.

Schools can play their part by working more systematically in a spirit of genuine collaboration

Teachers and school leaders are often reluctant to accept that they have a rather narrow view of the wider world, but working in schools can certainly lead to 'tunnel vision'. This can be helped by opening up to the power of collaboration between schools and also with business, charities and other groups and individuals in the community. This needs to be built into schools' improvement plans rather than being simply an aspiration. It will allow schools to be genuinely twenty-first century institutions which reflect modern thinking. The danger of not opening up to this wider world is that institutionalised thinking can result in repeated 'dead ends' during problem-solving. Students will then only suffer.

The government can play its part by facilitating collaboration between schools

There are some good examples of schemes that encourage schools to work together, such as the Independent–State School Partnerships. These should be expanded through more bursaries that allow schools to work together to address shared issues of concern. Similarly, the work of the regional Education Business Partnerships provide models of effective cross-sector work, yet some partnerships have had to be scaled back due to lack of funding in recent years. Such support is vital for schools if they are to benefit from outside expertise and the government can help by injecting new funds into this work.

Wider society can play its part by encouraging schools to learn from each other and by working with schools more actively

Many parents already take an active interest in the transition work of different schools when their children move up from primary to secondary school. This can be extended by following closely the wider collaborative work of schools, including their work with organisations outside school. Schools can be asked to publish details of their formal and informal links with others, thereby focusing their minds in this key aspect of their work. People working outside education can aid the bridge-building process with schools, helping them to make new links with businesses and charities.

8. We will cherish and promote creativity and innovation within our schools, for learners as well as for teachers, leaders and support staff

One of the most powerful messages contained in the stories in this book is that in each school success was only made possible by several creative leaps of imagination. Those school leaders, teachers and students interviewed all recognised that to achieve success, a certain amount of controlled risk taking—and even a little bit of outright experimentation—was central to the progress made. Despite firm messages from government that such innovation is valued, the plethora of initiatives, sometimes heavy-handed inspections and general feeling of oppressive control that can pervade the education system are not conducive to the vast majority of school leaders and teachers expressing their creativity. The fact that a school leader is still seen as a bit of a maverick for being prepared to use highly creative approaches suggests that we've currently got the balance wrong. Although we are at last beginning to see the government take its foot off the accelerator of new initiatives, and accept for the first time in a decade that schools must be allowed to innovate at a local level, more needs to be done at a variety of levels to promote the creative approaches that will bring more schools the success they currently crave. The importance of creativity extends to students, of course, too, who need to have it modelled in their leaders and teachers if they are to value it themselves. A creative student is one that is well equipped for a variety of futures.

Schools can play their part by celebrating and promoting creativity as one of the key attributes of successful schools

Some schools, including several featured in this book, are using enterprise as a practical demonstration of how creativity can work in practice. Other schools are marking their students' creativity through special prize-giving ceremonies. For these schools, innovation is part of the ethos, binding together staff and students. Other schools can model this approach, thereby placing greater emphasis on creativity and its role in learning. School leaders and governors have a special role to play in creating the culture for creativity to blossom in their schools.

The government can play its part by encouraging schools to innovate and by documenting and sharing good practice more widely

The government can take some simple concrete measures to help schools recognise and celebrate creativity in all its forms. The annual teaching awards, for example, currently champion good practice in schools, but a category is not yet reserved for creative schools. Similarly, a scheme funded through the government's Innovation Unit supports schools that are investigating unusual approaches to contemporary education issues. It should be expanded, more effectively advertised and the successes shared more widely. As there is a growing fashion for national 'champions' in the areas the government values, why not appoint a Schools Creativity Champion? All these measures will help to demonstrate that creativity really does matter in our schools.

Wider society can play its part by helping schools to find creative solutions

Creativity is stimulated by ideas, and these come from a variety of sources. Parents and other people working outside education can help schools to find creative solutions by lending their support to school initiatives. From being a governor to supporting the PTA there are many formal ways to get involved in the running of schools, together with a variety of less formal ones. All these roles need creative people and ideas.

9. We will stabilise funding to allow genuine long-term planning in our schools

For the last five years I've been supporting schools that wish to raise additional funds from *external* sources. While many schools have successfully augmented their budget using a range of tools and approaches, most are still left feeling that genuine long-term planning can only be possible if the funding arrangements for schools are stabilised. While we often encourage school leaders to envision a preferred future in three or five years' time, the unfortunate truth is that funding shortfalls or even changes to external funding often dictate the pace of positive change in many schools. The sentiment is summed up perfectly by the following notice which I saw pinned up in a staffroom: 'Wouldn't it be a wonderful day if we were provided with the money for our new community classroom and the RAF had to run jumble sales to afford their next bomber?' While recent government moves finally look set to address this, many school leaders still feel they are the 'have nots' when it comes to their funding.

Schools can play their part by recognising that long-term financial stability will enable success, while continuing to strive for additional external funding

Schools have become much more business-like in the last decade, with the role of the business manager or bursar becoming an integral part of many senior leadership teams. This has helped them to ensure they're providing best value through effective budget planning, but this cannot create long-term stability when there is simply not enough money to address all the priorities. Schools can tackle this conundrum by rigorous prioritisation, as well as continuing to seek external funds—there is over £1 billion a year now available. However, they should not shy away from applying continued pressure on local and national government to ensure additional and fairer funding for all schools.

The government can play its part by creating the long-term financial stability that so many schools crave

It took many years of Labour government before the mantra 'education, education, education' finally began to mean something in terms of funding. There is no doubt that schools in England are now better funded than ever before, but the uncertainties over budget allocations that have plagued schools for the last ten years still cause headteachers sleepless nights. The recent move to fix and guarantee budgets several years ahead will no doubt help, but the government can build on this to provide even more long-term stability for schools. This includes making it easier for *all* schools to become specialist schools, which brings with it over £500,000 in additional funding.

Wider society can play its part by pressuring the government to secure a stable financial future for schools that does not require them to go begging

Voter pressure can make a real difference on education matters, with political manifestos often replete with commitments in this critical area of public policy. Some parents might even be moved to write to their MP to secure a better financial future for their local school. Others might organise themselves in formal 'Fair funding for …' groups to provide greater leverage. While this pressure will no doubt help to move the government towards even greater stability of funding for schools, in the meantime parents and others can support schools' fundraising efforts in a variety of ways. This includes providing expert advice—or hands-on help—for a range of projects, as well as dipping into their own pockets during fundraising appeals.

10. *We will listen to the voice of young people in the running of our schools and open up to the power of their involvement*

Although there has been a reluctance by some schools to open up to the power of the student voice, many are now realising that genuine student involvement can be a wonderful tool for school improvement. Several of the case studies in this book demonstrate the hugely beneficial role that students can play in their schools, perhaps most notably in improving teaching and learning. In order for the views of young people to be taken more seriously in more schools, teachers, school leaders and the government all need to accept that in the past the role of students has been vastly underestimated. While this transition falls of short of handing over inappropriate amounts of power to students, the rather arrogant assumption that some educational professionals still cling to that 'students need to know their place' must be one of the first things to change.

Schools can play their part by accepting more readily the key role that students can play in school improvement

This can be done in very practical ways. It can begin by carrying out an audit which charts how students' views are currently represented at your school, and move on to a series of actions to develop better representation. Some schools have gone much further by appointing students as governors and using them systematically during the recruitment of teachers and even headteachers. This also needs to be tackled at the level of the culture of the school too, with those resistant to this positive change being challenged.

The government can play its part by providing a framework and active support for work to embrace the student voice in schools

As the government is sympathetic to this work, it follows that it should be doing much to champion the role of students in the running of schools. Unfortunately, this work is still in its infancy at the national level. A good practice website on the student voice, funded by the government, would go some way to filling this gap. New guidance for Ofsted inspectors on the extent to which the student voice is being used to promote school improvement would also add weight to this area of schools' practice.

Wider society can play its part by encouraging schools and the government to listen to the voice of students

Parents can help schools to make the transition to a more systematic use of students' views by encouraging their children to reflect on the school's strengths and weaknesses while at home. This needs to be done in a spirit of positive development rather than complaint! Parents can also comment on the use of the student voice during school inspections, signalling that this is considered important. For this change to take place, parents and other adults also need to accept that we do not really listen to the views of young people on a host of issues, never mind taking on board their ideas. Work to address this can begin in the home as much as it can in schools.

Where does the majority influence lie?

	Schools	Government	Wider society
School leaders will be skilled in leadership and teaching and learning in equal proportion.	**	**	*
School leaders and teachers will be trusted as highly trained professionals.	*	**	**
An overall framework to help schools succeed will be provided, but this will also allow them to innovate to find appropriate local solutions.	*	**	*
We will let go of the notion that continual, short-term major change is beneficial to schools and learners.	*	**	*
We will accept that the national obsession with tests, targets and examinations is not producing learners with the knowledge and skills to thrive in the uncertain world of tomorrow.	*	**	*

	Schools	Government	Wider society
We will stand up for what really matters in our schools—creating happy, resourceful and well-educated students equipped with lifelong thinking and learning skills.	* *	*	* *
Schools will learn from each other in order to avoid 'institutionalised' thinking.	* *	*	* *
We will cherish and promote creativity and innovation within our schools, for learners as well as for teachers, leaders and support staff.	* *	* *	*
We will stabilise funding to allow genuine long-term planning in our schools.	*	* *	*
We will listen to the voice of young people in the running of our schools and open up to the power of their involvement.	* *	* *	*

What are the implications of this manifesto?

I bring this section to an end by considering what my 'manifesto for real change in our schools' means for you—whatever your role. There are some key principles that emerge from the ten points of the manifesto, including some that are relevant for us all. If positive change is to really take place in our schools, then people need to recognise that they have the power to make a difference and understand what they need to do.

Key implications

For everyone

Accepting our role

- We all must recognise that we can play our part in transforming schools for the better—and this will help transform the life prospects of young people
- We must engage in debates and dialogue with others about education matters in a spirit of openness
- We must all play our part in helping schools to become more collaborative and outward-looking—with other schools and with businesses, charities and other facets of the world outside the school gates

Recognising what schools are for

- We should accept that schools are ultimately places for learning, where the focus is on the whole person
- We must be very clear what our personal vision for education is and what needs to be done for it to be realised

Celebrating what will bring success

- We must celebrate creative approaches to education that use fresh approaches to tackle deep-seated challenges
- We must encourage a much more systematic use of students' views and ideas to improve practice in their schools

- We must all help teachers to be seen as highly qualified, professional people, carrying out one of the most important jobs in society
- We must all work for more stability in the funding of schools, with increased spending on the things that matter most in schools
- We must cherish the profound long-term changes that will really help to improve schools, rather than focusing on continual short-term change and shallow initiatives

For school leaders and governors

- They must accept the responsibility that comes with the more flexible educational framework for schools that lies ahead
- They must understand the need for a balance between a national framework for the work of schools and local innovation to meet specific needs
- They must take full responsibility for the highest standards of educational leadership and management in their schools
- They should commit to making creativity a key part of the ethos of their schools

For teachers

- They must take full responsibility for the highest standards of teaching and learning in their classrooms
- They must be fully committed to continued development in their careers through a variety of training routes
- They should accept that increasing autonomy will bring with it accountability for their teaching pedagogies

For parents

- They must commit to educating themselves about some of the key issues underpinning the work of schools, thereby enabling them to engage in more informed debate

- Where possible, they should get involved in the workings of schools, using their knowledge and skills to add value
- They should be prepared to lobby MPs, the government and others, and use their democratic rights as voters to influence decision-making about schools

For students

- They must take responsibility for their learning as well as enjoying their rights as learners
- They must rise to the challenge of being a student in a time a rapid change—and recognise that the world of tomorrow will be different still
- They must involve themselves in decision-making in their schools

For business and community leaders

- They must recognise that they possess vital skills and knowledge that can help schools to become more effective
- They should commit to sharing their knowledge and skills by working actively with schools at a variety of levels
- They should work with students in classrooms, while accepting that teachers are the experts in facilitating learning

For the government

- They must maintain the focus on excellence in schools, while opening up to the power that comes with freedom, flexibility and responsiveness to local circumstances
- They should begin a national debate on what really matters in our schools with the aim of building a powerful consensus on the way forward
- They should appoint a schools Creativity Champion and a children's Happiness Tsar to tackle these two critical areas of education

What's your manifesto for change?

As you read my manifesto, I hope you too were stimulated to consider what your own 'manifesto for real change' in our schools would look like. In fact, I urge you to create one within a month of reading the book, as well as encouraging your colleagues, friends and relatives to do the same. Together, perhaps we can provide a powerful, united voice for positive change in our schools—creating a future where all schools enjoy the success of those featured in this book.

We cannot allow the young people in our schools to miss out on their only opportunity: many more of our schools need to be exhilarating places in which to learn. The possibilities of change are indeed exciting but we need to picture what our preferred future might look like—then we must work tirelessly together to make that vision a reality. Future generations might find it hard to forgive us if we cannot say we were part of creating that brighter future.

What will be the first thing that you will do?

About the author

Brin Best is an education consultant specialising in teaching and learning and school improvement. He enjoyed a distinguished record as a teacher, head of department and local authority advisory teacher, receiving several national awards and prizes for his work. This included a Millennium Fellowship for his pioneering work on environmental education.

His company, Innovation *for* Education Ltd, works in partnership with teachers and school leaders to secure a brighter future for our young people. Brin trains or works in a one to one role with hundreds of education professionals every year. His twin passions for creativity and the possibilities of change permeate all his work.

Brin is also an award-winning education author, with fifteen previous books to his name, spanning classroom issues and the management of schools. He also writes for newspapers, professional publications for teachers and learned journals. He is the co-originator and series consultant for the highly acclaimed *Teachers' Pocketbooks*.

Brin maintains a keen research interest in education issues. He is carrying out part-time doctoral studies into effective teaching and learning approaches at Leeds University and is working with PGCE and masters students on a range of subjects.

Brin enjoys wilderness, exploration and natural history. He was elected a Fellow of the Royal Geographical Society following his expeditions to the Ecuadorian Andes. He is very active in the charity sector and is a trustee of the Royal Society for the Protection of Birds, Europe's largest environmental organisation.

He can be contacted via brinbest@hotmail.com

Further reading and information

Best, Brin and Thomas, Will, *The Creative Teaching & Learning Toolkit* (Continuum International Publishing, 2007)

Butler, Kathleen, *Learning and Teaching Style: In Theory and Practice* (Hawker Brownlow, 1993)

Fink, Dean, *Leadership for Mortals: Developing and Sustaining Leaders of Learning* (Leading Teachers, Leading Schools Series) (Paul Chapman, 2005)

Ginnis, Paul, *The Teacher's Toolkit: Raise Classroom Achievement with Strategies for Every Learner* (Crown House, 2001)

Kagan, Spencer, *Cooperative Learning* (Kagan Publishing, 2001)

Wise, Derek and Lovatt, Mark, *Creating an Accelerated Learning School.* (Network Educational Press, 2001)

Wiseman, Richard, *The Luck Factor: The Scientific Study of the Lucky Mind* (Arrow Books, 2004)

Training courses and workshops on creativity across the curriculum are available through www.creativityforlearning.co.uk

Index

A
Able student 82, 129, 194, 195
Accelerated learning 110
Achievements 7, 34, 76, 87, 119, 122, 125, 149, 154, 161, 168, 189, 209
Age Concern 28, 29, 33, 41
Aptitude 85
Assessment 59, 82, 83, 86, 87, 100, 133, 198
Attention 18, 39, 40, 68, 75, 92, 111, 119, 140, 158, 186

B
Barriers 111, 183, 204, 207
 internal and external 223
 to innovation 5, 221–226, 227
Behaviour 83–85, 104, 183, 204, 209
Brain-based learning 190
Budgets 169, 211, 228, 243
Bullying 73, 173

C
Challenges 7, 9, 27, 39, 42, 46, 48, 49, 68, 76, 84, 90, 99, 101, 111, 124, 141, 144, 148, 151, 161, 175, 177, 179, 183, 195, 196, 202, 204, 210, 213, 214, 224, 225, 230, 248
Clarke, Chris 45, 65, 74
Collaboration 41, 46, 60, 114, 159, 161, 164, 174–177, 179, 191, 217, 239, 240
Comenius programme 168, 170
Community partners 133, 134
Communications strategy 37
Concept 105, 137, 203, 218, 232
Continuing Professional Development (CPD) (*see also* professional development) 74, 81, 124, 217, 230
Cooperation 161, 179
Corporate 149
Creativity/creative 10, 34, 38, 40, 43, 46, 48, 78, 96, 104, 105, 107, 112, 119, 125, 134, 142, 147, 149, 158, 171, 178, 185, 186, 189, 194, 200, 203, 210, 214–217, 219, 222, 223, 225, 226, 239–242, 247–250
Culture 42, 49, 79, 96, 101, 105, 107, 110, 122–125, 130–132, 135, 137, 138, 140, 145, 150, 154, 158, 170, 204, 208, 210, 235, 236, 239, 241, 245
Curriculum 24, 39, 48, 49, 62, 68, 70, 83, 88, 92, 96, 99, 105, 106, 133, 134, 140, 141, 154, 171, 196, 224, 225, 230, 232
Enriched 85

D
Data poor 86
Data rich 86
Dedication 83, 183, 189, 210
Deming, W. Edwards 106
Department for Education and Skills (DfES) 167, 171
Disabilities 91, 92
Discipline 34
Discussion 30, 68, 71, 87, 90, 91, 109, 117, 118, 132, 136, 141, 237

Drivers 43, 205, 213, 214, 218
    Characteristics 210, 213, 219
    External 217
    Growing 216, 217
    Managing 215
    Whole school 214, 216

E

Education business partnerships (*see also* partnership) 141, 148, 240
Email 61, 170
Engage 39, 46, 68, 105, 112, 134, 152, 183, 203, 219, 228, 231, 232, 248, 249
Enterprise 129-158, 170, 171, 178, 238, 241
Enterprise learning 136, 141
Enthusiasm 6, 23, 36, 40, 73, 104, 138, 139, 152, 153, 156, 158, 183, 185, 190, 202
Environment Fair 10, 11, 19, 39, 41
Evaluation 30, 134, 168, 221
Every Child Matters 137, 172
Excellence 44, 68, 70, 73, 81, 103, 127, 149, 158, 202, 250
Exclusion 84, 99
Expectation 99, 106, 167, 179, 182, 185, 193, 201, 202, 204, 208, 210, 230, 239
Extended Schools 39
External relationships 154
External speakers 140, 141

F

Feedback 39, 82, 114, 117, 118, 124, 155, 167, 191-194, 198, 230
Financial stability 243
Flexibility 134, 221, 232, 250
Forward planning 156

Frederick Soddy Trust 20, 21, 25
Fun 12, 13, 60, 65, 71, 96, 237
Funding 5, 10, 20, 21, 29, 40, 68, 155, 164, 166-169, 171, 172, 174, 175, 177, 178, 196, 240, 242-245, 247
Fundraising 21, 28, 41, 147, 180, 244

G

GCSE 12, 20, 50, 56, 80, 84-86, 89, 109, 137, 139, 140, 151, 182, 183, 186, 188, 190, 192-195, 198
Geography 8, 10, 13, 20, 23, 55, 191, 192-194, 203
Ginnis, Paul 111, 119
Goals 3, 5, 10, 43, 49, 73, 88, 126, 180, 208-210, 214, 218, 220, 224, 232, 238
Good practice 3, 6, 87, 111-113, 165, 171, 191, 192, 198, 200, 212, 215, 239, 241, 242, 245
Governors 38, 40, 189, 228, 234, 241, 245, 249
Government initiatives 88, 100, 107, 122, 234, 237
Gregorc, Anthony 110

H

Hayes, Jarvis 7, 129
History 54, 71, 103, 104
Homework 61, 186
Humanities 105, 116, 120, 165

I

ICT 4, 36, 45-58, 60-66, 69, 71-76, 82, 133, 134, 138, 146, 150, 151, 154-157, 189, 190
Implications 186, 212, 234, 248
    School leaders 249
    Teachers 249

Parents 249
Students 226, 250
Business/community 250
Government 250
Inclusion 91, 92, 96, 98, 133, 137
Independent 234
Innovation 5, 99, 107, 109, 123, 139, 147, 149, 155, 157, 159, 210, 213, 221–223, 227, 240–242, 247, 249
INSET 51, 53, 55, 57, 59, 148, 149, 153, 171
Investing 81, 99

K
Key Stage(s) 48, 137, 154
Key Stage 3 50, 52, 60, 61, 109, 111, 144, 145, 150, 151, 171
Key Stage 4 85, 140, 152, 167, 196
Kimble, Richard 142

L
Language 79, 104, 109, 110, 121, 122, 143, 165, 170, 195
Leadership 43, 45, 65, 66, 68, 69, 82, 91, 98–100, 103, 106, 107, 109, 112, 125, 126, 131, 156, 157, 179, 188, 194–196, 200, 208, 209, 211, 218–220, 228, 229, 243, 246, 249
League tables 70, 224, 236
Learning environment 60, 64, 71, 197
Learning to Learn 111, 117, 119, 191, 201, 237
Lesson planning 142–144
Lifelong learning 33, 39, 76, 124, 133

M
Manifesto 6, 224, 227, 248, 251
Millennium map 20, 24–26, 41

Mission statement 131–133, 135
Modern languages 66, 133, 134, 137
Moodle 57–60, 62, 63
Monitoring 86, 89, 98, 136, 201
  and evaluation 168, 221
Motivate 80, 113, 137

N
National College for School Leadership (NCSL) 109, 228, 229
National Curriculum 39, 224, 225
National Enterprise Network 153
National Foundation for Educational Research (NFER) 229
Newsletter(s) 17, 19, 21, 23, 27, 28, 33, 36, 37, 39, 45, 51, 88, 113, 153
'no blame' culture 107, 124

O
Ofsted 66, 70, 83, 192, 245
One-to-one coaching 81
Operational factors 208, 211
Outcomes 86, 126, 136, 137, 170, 175, 178, 179, 201, 217

P
Parents 8, 11, 41, 62, 63, 78, 84, 87–89, 96, 102, 153–155, 179, 189, 191, 212, 224, 229, 233, 235–238, 240, 242, 244, 245, 249
Participate 11, 113, 170
Partnership (see also *education and education business*) 64, 73, 85, 88, 92, 96, 113, 133, 141, 150, 159, 161, 240
PE 10, 85, 182, 185, 186, 189
Peer 173
Performing arts 38, 66, 71, 168, 169, 171, 173, 190

Personalise 85
Pressures 4, 42, 109, 177, 195, 224, 225
Problem-solving 134, 142, 149, 152, 226, 238, 239
Professional development 81, 83, 99, 112, 118, 210, 229
Professionalism 188, 189, 230, 231
Progress 6, 64, 78, 84, 86, 87, 91, 99, 101, 107, 110, 136, 148, 149, 155, 161, 174, 191, 197, 204, 205, 213, 221, 228, 233, 238, 241

R
Real life learning 11, 39
Relationships 40, 61, 78, 81, 132, 141, 154, 155
Risk taking 123, 125, 191, 192, 203, 240
Roles
  of individuals & groups 156, 242
  of students 171
  of teachers 4, 123
Royal Geographical Society 20, 25

S
School improvement 82, 98, 177, 217, 218, 221, 223, 234, 244, 245
Science 10, 54, 55, 71, 78, 80, 85, 111, 137, 165, 196, 197, 200, 201
Secrets of success 38, 74, 97, 122, 154, 177, 201
Self-confidence 134
Self-discipline 106
Self-image 124
Settle environment fair (see Environment Fair)
Schemes of work (see also Lesson planning) 141–144, 150, 151, 156

Special educational needs 91, 92
Specialist School Trust 153
Staff
  turnover 83
  training (see also teacher training and INSET) 48, 53, 55, 56, 66, 80, 81, 99, 112–114, 117, 124–126, 148, 149, 171, 190, 229, 230, 232, 233, 249
Stimulus 71, 105
Strategy 37, 58, 63, 87, 109, 111, 125, 169, 174, 209, 220, 221, 234
Student:
  council 72, 96
  empowerment 42, 173, 178
  involvement 122, 169, 244
  observers 109, 113, 114, 117, 118, 124
  progress 86
  voice 73, 96, 113, 124, 172, 244, 245
Subject expertise 75
Sustainability 134, 171, 175, 178

T
Teacher training 81, 112, 124
Teachers' TV 58, 71
Teamwork 39, 70, 110, 142, 179
Testing 72, 224, 235, 236
Thinking
  'insitutionalised' 239, 247
  positively 100
  skills 201, 237, 247
Times Educational Supplement (TES) 19, 56, 93
Timetabling 59, 87, 156
Transferable 43, 75, 101, 126, 157, 179, 204
Trust 100, 132, 229–231, 234

U
Underachievement 87, 89, 98, 164, 192, 195
University of the Third Age 153

V
Variety 29, 58, 109, 119, 124, 147, 153, 169, 182, 189, 207, 219, 220, 241, 242, 244, 249, 250
Virtual Learning Environment (VLE) 57, 60, 62
Vision 10, 20, 28, 41, 63, 75, 91, 107, 119, 131, 132, 135, 154, 158, 171, 176, 179, 208, 209, 211, 221, 224, 230, 233–235, 248, 251
Vocational 80, 85, 88, 139, 171
Voice of students 245

W
Wonderwall 200